Much Ado About Nothing

by William Shakespeare

Michael Jones

Series Editors:
Sue Bennett and Dave Stockwin

HODDER
EDUCATION
AN HACHETTE UK COMPANY

The Publishers would like to thank the following for permission to reproduce copyright material.

Photo credits

p. 8 © Shakespeare's Globe Photo library, Manuel Harlan, 2011 production; **p. 11** Fotolia; **p. 19** © Shakespeare's Globe Photo library, John Tramper, 2004 production; **p. 21** © Shakespeare's Globe Photo library, Andy Bradshaw, 2008 production; **p. 24** © Shakespeare's Globe Photo library, John Tramper, 2004 production; **p. 26** © Shakespeare's Globe Photo library, Manuel Harlan, 2011 production; **p. 29** © Shakespeare's Globe Photo library, John Tramper, 2004 production; **p. 41** TopFoto; **p. 42** TopFoto; **p. 45** Moviestore Collection Ltd/Alamy; **p. 51** ZUMA Press, Inc./Alamy

Every effort has been made to trace all copyright holders, but if any have been inadvertently overlooked, the Publishers will be pleased to make the necessary arrangements at the first opportunity.

Although every effort has been made to ensure that website addresses are correct at time of going to press, Hodder Education cannot be held responsible for the content of any website mentioned in this book. It is sometimes possible to find a relocated web page by typing in the address of the home page for a website in the URL window of your browser.

Hachette UK's policy is to use papers that are natural, renewable and recyclable products and made from wood grown in sustainable forests. The logging and manufacturing processes are expected to conform to the environmental regulations of the country of origin.

Orders: please contact Bookpoint Ltd, 130 Park Drive, Milton Park, Abingdon, Oxon OX14 4SE. Telephone: (44) 01235 827720. Fax: (44) 01235 400454. Email education@bookpoint.co.uk Lines are open from 9 a.m. to 5 p.m., Monday to Saturday, with a 24-hour message answering service. You can also order through our website: www.hoddereducation.co.uk

ISBN: 978 1 4718 5363 0

© Michael Jones, 2016

First published in 2016 by

Hodder Education,

An Hachette UK Company

Carmelite House

50 Victoria Embankment

London EC4Y 0DZ

www.hoddereducation.co.uk

Impression number	10 9 8 7 6 5 4 3 2 1
Year	2020 2019 2018 2017 2016

Cover photo © Raisa Kanareva/Getty Images/Hemera/Thinkstock

Illustrations by Integra Software Services Pvt. Ltd

Typeset in 11/13pt Bliss Light by Integra Software Services Pvt. Ltd., Pondicherry, India

Printed in Italy

A catalogue record for this title is available from the British Library.

Contents

Getting the most from this guide

This guide is designed to help you raise your achievement in your examination response to *Much Ado About Nothing*. It is intended for you to use throughout your GCSE English Literature course. It will help you when you are studying the play for the first time and also during your revision.

The following features have been used throughout this guide to help you focus your understanding of the play:

Target your thinking

A list of **introductory questions** labelled by Assessment Objective is provided at the beginning of each chapter to give you a breakdown of the material covered. They target your thinking, in order to help you work more efficiently by focusing on the key messages.

Build critical skills

These boxes offer an opportunity to consider some **more challenging questions**. They are designed to encourage deeper thinking, analysis and exploratory thought. Building and practising critical skills in this way will give you a real advantage in the examination.

GRADE *FOCUS*

It is possible to know a play well and yet still underachieve in the examination if you are unsure what the examiners are looking for. The **GRADE FOCUS** boxes give a clear explanation of **how you may be assessed**, with an emphasis on the criteria for gaining a Grade 5 and a Grade 8.

REVIEW YOUR LEARNING

At the end of each chapter you will find this section to **test your knowledge**: a series of short, specific questions to ensure you have understood and absorbed the key messages of the section. Answers to the 'Review your learning' questions are provided in the final section of the guide (p. 102).

GRADE *BOOSTER*

Read and remember these pieces of helpful **grade-boosting advice**. They provide top tips from experienced teachers and examiners who can advise you on what to do, as well as what *not* to do, in order to maximise your chances of success in the examination.

Key quotation

Key quotations are highlighted for you, so that if you wish you may use them as **supporting evidence** in your examination answers. Further quotations, grouped by characterisation, theme and the author's methods, can be found in the 'Top ten' section on page 95 of the guide. All page references in this guide refer to the 2014 edition of *Much Ado About Nothing*, published by Cambridge School Shakespeare (ISBN 978-1-107-61989-0). '2.1 14–15' means 'Act 2 scene 1 lines 14–15'.

'Give not this rotten orange to your friend.'
(4.1 27)

Introduction

Studying the text

You may find it useful to read sections of this guide when you need them, rather than reading it from start to finish. For example, assuming that you have read or seen the play itself, the section on 'Context' might be a good place to start since it offers an explanation of the relevant historical, cultural and literary background to the play. It is here where you will find information about aspects of Shakespeare's life and times which influenced his writing, the particular issues with which Shakespeare was concerned and where the play stands in terms of the literary tradition of which it is part.

As you work through the play, you may find it helpful to read the relevant 'Plot and structure' sections before or after studying a particular act or scene. As well as a summary of events there is also critical commentary, so that you are aware of how Shakespeare presents the unfolding drama. The sections on 'Characterisation', 'Themes', and 'Language, style and analysis' will help to develop your thinking further, in preparation for written responses on particular aspects of the text.

An initial reading of the section on 'Assessment Objectives and skills' will enable you to make really effective notes in preparation for assessments. The Assessment Objectives are what examination boards base their mark schemes on. In this section they are broken down and clearly explained.

Revising the text

Whether you study the play in a block of time close to the exam or much earlier in your GCSE Literature course, you will need to revise thoroughly if you are to achieve the very best grade that you can.

You should first remind yourself of what happens in the play and so the chapter on 'Plot and structure' might be returned to in the first instance. You might then look at the 'Assessment Objectives' section to ensure that you understand what the examiners are looking for in general, and then look carefully at the 'Tackling the exams' section. This section gives you useful information on question format, depending on which examination board specification you are following, as well as advice on the examination format, and practical considerations such as the time available for the question and the Assessment Objectives which apply to it.

Advice is also supplied on how to approach the question, how to create a quick plan and how to produce an effective answer. There is focused advice on how you might improve your grade, so you need to read this section carefully. You might also have fun inventing and answering additional questions since you can be sure that the ones in the sample materials will not be the ones you see when you open the exam paper!

With most examination boards the Shakespeare question is based on an extract and is in two parts: you will be asked to write in detail about an extract before writing about an aspect of the play as a whole. With some boards, such as AQA, the aspect you need to focus on in the second part will feature in the extract, but in other boards the general question may not be so directly related to the extract. Whichever board you are sitting you need to become familiar with the format and timing of the paper and to have practised planning and writing answers in the time available.

You will find examples of exam-style responses in the 'Sample essays' section, with examiner comments in the margins, so that you can see clearly how to achieve a Grade 5 and how to then move from Grade 5 to Grade 8.

Now that all GCSE Literature examinations are 'closed book', the 'Top ten' section offers you the opportunity to learn short quotations to support points about ten top character and theme moments and about Shakespeare's techniques. There are also suggestions for wider reading.

This guide is not a substitute for your own studying of *Much Ado About Nothing* but it should help you to clarify your thinking about the play and it should also help you to consolidate your approach to writing well under the pressure of the examination. The suggestions in the guide can help you to develop habits of planning and writing answers that take the worry out of *how* you write, and so enable you to concentrate on *what* you write.

Remember: the examiners are not looking for set responses. You should not read this guide in order to memorise chunks of it, ready to regurgitate in the exam. Identical answers are dull. The examiners hope to reward you for perceptive thought, individual appreciation and awareness of varying interpretations. They want to sense that you have enjoyed engaging with the themes and ideas in *Much Ado About Nothing*, and explored Shakespeare's methods with an awareness of the context in which he wrote.

Enjoying Shakespeare

Much Ado About Nothing is still a popular play, with much to say to modern audiences about the relationships between men and women and the danger of mistaking appearance for reality. However it is also a play which is full of Elizabethan jokes and references that make some aspects of its humour difficult for a modern audience to appreciate. For example, the play is full of jokes about fashion at the end of the sixteenth century.

Unless you have seen photographs of the 2004 Globe Theatre production or a performance in Elizabethan costume it might be hard to appreciate just how elaborate Elizabethan costumes were for the men and boys playing male and female characters.

Every performance of a play is a director's interpretation of what Shakespeare wrote. Try to see (in the theatre or on film) more than one version of *Much Ado About Nothing*. (See page 101 for a suggested film version.) If possible try to see the play in the Globe Theatre since that is the best way to gain a sense of what the theatres were like in Shakespeare's time. As a minimum, if visiting the Globe Theatre itself is not possible, do an internet search for 'the Globe Theatre' and look at photographs and/or drawings to see how the stage was arranged and how the audience would have been seated.

▲ A 2011 production of the play at the Globe Theatre

Each performance is a reflection of its own time as well as of the time when Shakespeare wrote the play. For example, in a modern performance you would pick up a director's intention to reflect contemporary ideas about the rights of women because you are familiar with such ideas, but it is more of a challenge for you to identify Shakespeare's original intentions. The more you understand about Elizabethan ideas and the expectations of Elizabethan audiences the more you are able to appreciate what Shakespeare was trying to do. In a play like *Much Ado About Nothing*, which the audience knew was a comedy, there might be near-tragic elements (and there are) but it has to end in marriage and merriment.

Shakespeare is not recognised as the world's greatest playwright for nothing: his plays have extraordinary power and have given extraordinary pleasure to audiences across time and across the world. Try not to let the pressure of being examined on Shakespeare spoil your lifetime's enjoyment of his plays. For many people, and you may be one, the more they know about a play the more they enjoy it.

Enjoy referring to the guide as you study the text and good luck in your exam.

Context

Target your thinking

- What do examiners mean by 'context'? (**AO3**)
- How can awareness of the historical and literary context deepen your understanding of the play? (**AO1, AO3**)
- Which aspects and attitudes of Elizabethan times are relevant to the play? (**AO3**)
- How might audiences in different times see different ideas and issues in the play? (**AO3**)

What is meant by 'context'?

Context (AO3) in GCSE English Literature is a complex term. It has five different aspects:

- **The historical context:** the relationship between the ideas and events in the play and the time when the play was written.
- **The literary context:** other texts and traditions of which the playwright was aware.
- **The context of the text:** where and when the play was set by the playwright.
- **The audience context:** ways in which interpretation and audience response reflect the different times and places in which the play is performed.
- **The performance context:** every performance (on stage or screen) is a director's interpretation of what Shakespeare wrote. A key decision by a director is where and when to set the play.

The good news is that GCSE examiners do not want you to reel off information about Shakespeare's life and times – what they want is for you to use your knowledge of Elizabethan society and ideas to deepen your understanding of *Much Ado About Nothing*. You do not need to write about Shakespeare's life, which is just as well since we know remarkably little about the life of the world's most famous playwright.

The play's the thing, but what is a play? A script, a performance or a film? For you, a twenty-first century student preparing to be examined on *Much Ado About Nothing,* probably all three. For Shakespeare it would have been a performance, since he made his money from his theatre company's performances and his plays were not published properly until after his death.

Shakespeare the man

Shakespeare was born in Stratford in 1564 and went to the local grammar school. He married Anne Hathaway in 1582 when he was eighteen and Anne (already pregnant) was in her twenties. They had three children, two girls and a boy. The boy, Hamnet, died aged eleven. Shakespeare's family remained in Stratford, but by 1592, when he was in his late twenties, he was living in London and starting to gain recognition as a poet and playwright. He had a remarkably successful career during which his plays were performed at court and (often) in the Globe Theatre. He became a partner (shareholder) in the theatre company that was called the Lord Chamberlain's Men which (from 1603) became known as the King's Men because of the patronage of the new King James I. He moved back to Stratford in around 1611 and died there in 1616.

Shakespeare the playwright

Shakespeare wrote 37 plays, some of them in collaboration with other dramatists. Surprisingly to us, despite his reputation there was no collected edition of his plays until after his death.

In the 1580s and 1590s theatregoers did not expect total originality. Shakespeare followed the usual practice of basing his plays on historical sources or earlier plays. His first comedy (*The Comedy of Errors*) was based on a play by the Roman writer Plautus, and most of his plays that followed were based on stories from other texts. What is interesting for a modern audience is how he developed from those starting points. In *Much Ado About Nothing* the story of a maid impersonating her mistress would have been known to Shakespeare from Edmund Spenser's *Faerie Queene*, but the most dramatically interesting characters are the ones that Shakespeare invented – Beatrice, Benedick and Dogberry. None of these characters is in his main source, which was a story by Italian Matteo Bandello written nearly fifty years earlier, nor in the various versions of similar stories that Shakespeare might have known and drawn upon.

Shakespeare's theatre

Much Ado About Nothing was written around 1598. This was a time when the London theatres were popular but under increasing threat from Puritan pressure groups seeking to limit the number of theatres and performances.

Theatre-going in Shakespeare's day (and it usually was daytime) was not the respectable experience it so often is today. Ordinary people (the 'groundlings') paid a penny to enter and stood in the yard (known

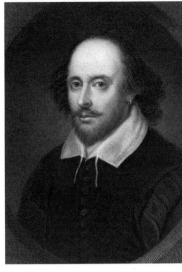

▲ Shakespeare

Build critical skills

Beatrice rages against 'her' femininity:

Oh God that I were a man! I would eat his heart in the market place.

(4.1 294)

How might the reactions of an Elizabethan audience have been influenced by the fact that 'she' was played by a boy not a woman?

as the pit) in front of the stage in the open, as in today's reconstructed Globe Theatre. Wealthier patrons sat on benches under cover, overlooking the pit and the stage.

Elizabethan audiences did not listen in respectful silence: they drank, ate, shouted and interrupted as they saw fit. Plays were much more like our pantomimes than like today's serious plays, which tend to have well-behaved, middle-aged, middle-class audiences.

All the actors were men or boys – women were not allowed to perform on stage. The impact of having male actors playing Hero and Beatrice is hard for many modern audiences to envisage, but it does change the way gender relations are presented. The theatre depends on what the critic S. T. Coleridge once called 'the willing suspension of disbelief': imagining Southwark as Sicily is as much of a challenge as forgetting that the woman on stage is a boy acting as a woman. As you will know, a number of modern TV shows feature men as women (for example, Brendan O'Carroll as the mother in *Mrs Brown's Boys*) and almost every pantomime has a female as 'Principal Boy'.

There was little by way of scenery or props, so playwrights set their scenes through the words of their characters. Performance was continuous – the division into acts and scenes is the work of later editors rather than of Shakespeare himself.

Shakespeare's England

The England of Shakespeare's day is present in *Much Ado About Nothing* through characters, imagery and ideas about society.

The Elizabethan Watch

Some of the characters Shakespeare invented, such as Dogberry, Verges and the Watch, are drawn from contemporary life in England. There was no professional police force, so the maintenance of good order depended on magistrates, elected (but unpaid) constables and citizens who acted as nightwatchmen – the Watch. They were notoriously corrupt and ineffective – as one of the Watch observes, 'we know what belongs to a watch' (3.3 33) and essentially that meant avoiding trouble rather than dealing with crime. It is possible that Dogberry, first played by Will Kempe, the famous clown of Shakespeare's company, was modelled on an actual constable, but what matters is that Shakespeare's audience would have recognised the stereotype of the bumbling, incompetent but self-important constable. What distinguishes Dogberry from any conventional type is of course his magnificently mangled language. It is part of Shakespeare's humour, as well as his ideas, that the Watch do discover the wrongdoing – a rare occurrence in Elizabethan England.

Key quotation

Dogberry's advice:

the most peaceable way for you, if you do take a thief, is, to let him show himself what he is, and steal out of your company.
(3.3 48–50)

It is important to have some knowledge of Shakespeare's times. This will help you to understand his purposes and concerns as well as any contemporary issues which may have affected the presentation of characters or themes. However, there is little to be gained by simply 'bolting on' biographical or cultural details. They must always be related to the question you are answering.

Fathers, then and now

Fathers in Shakespeare don't generally come out looking good, particularly to modern audiences. Like Leonato, many follow Elizabethan convention in assuming that they can control their daughters' lives and feelings. Antonio expresses the general (male) view in saying 'I trust you will be ruled by your father' (2.1 38). When their wishes are thwarted, the fathers, such as Lord Capulet in *Romeo and Juliet,* tend to berate their daughters beyond all reason, as Leonato does with Hero until doubt creeps in that she might have been 'belied'.

Elizabethan society

Society in Messina reflects society in Elizabethan England: noble families have the power and influence while the lower orders have roles as servants or citizens. Shakespeare chose to show that these two layers of society are connected – the humble Watch reveal the evil of Don John, who, despite being born a bastard (i.e. to parents not married to each other), is deemed to be of noble birth.

Like Messina, the Elizabethan world was largely, but not wholly, a man's world. Shakespeare chose to create Beatrice as a woman capable of challenging male domination with her sharp wit and her belief that women have the right to think for themselves. She mocks the military prowess of Benedick and is the first to realise that the noblemen are confidently wrong about what they have seen. She also declares that women should choose their marriage partners: '…say, father, as it please me' (2.1 41) and thereby challenges the conventional Elizabethan assumption that, especially among noble families, marriage was a matter of family alliances rather than personal affection.

Elizabethan fashion

Fashion mattered to Elizabethans, and clothing was an elaborate reflection of Elizabethan society: as a rule the richer the clothing the richer the person, so no-one was more elaborately dressed than Queen Elizabeth herself, shown in her portraits as arrayed in pearls and in cloth-of-gold that only royal personages could wear.

thou knowest that the fashion of a doublet, or a hat, or a cloak, is nothing to a man.

(Borachio, 3.3 96–97)

How does Borachio's tirade against the 'deformed thief' fashion link with Shakespeare's theme of appearance and reality?

Unsurprisingly, *Much Ado About Nothing* abounds with references to clothing and fashion, since fashion is one way that people disguise or conceal their true selves: in the opening scene Beatrice equates Benedick's faith and fashion as things that he can change on a whim. The most extended reference to fashion is Borachio's diatribe: 'See'st thou not what a deformed thief this fashion is?' (3.3 107). Shakespeare's point is not just that fashions deform the human body (as Elizabethan fashions certainly did) but that outward appearance is often seen as more significant than inner worth, which is what has just happened with Margaret's impersonation of Hero. The nobles are deceived by clothing – Margaret wears Hero's dress in the window – and this is part of Shakespeare's wider concern with deception. Elizabethan fashions were so elaborate that they deformed the human body and *Much Ado About Nothing* shows the audience that society's rules and attitudes can similarly deform the human spirit.

The language of Elizabethan times

Shakespeare's language naturally reflects the Elizabethan England in which he lived: it abounds in images that contemporaries would find familiar such as country life, birds (Claudio is 'a poor hurt fowl' [2.1 154] while Beatrice 'like a lapwing, runs' [3.1 24]), animals, pub signs, fencing and the exploration of new worlds such as Asia or the antipodes – Benedick says that rather than have to meet 'My Lady Tongue' (Beatrice) he would 'fetch you a tooth-picker now from the furthest inch of Asia' or 'fetch you a hair off the Great Cham's beard' (2.1 201–203).

It could be argued that the most highly charged words in the play are when Beatrice says, 'Kill Claudio!' Elizabethan gentlemen wore swords and duelling was part of Elizabethan life and death. If a gentleman's honour, or that of his lady, was at stake, the matter would be settled with swords rather than words.

Elizabethan attitudes

Shakespeare explores and challenges conventional Elizabethan assumptions about many aspects of society, notably the role of women. (See also the section on 'Themes', p. 44.)

- Unconventional Beatrice, the more appealing character on stage because of her spirited independence of mind and quickness of tongue, is a deliberate contrast with conventionally submissive Hero.
- Male confidence and arrogance, developed in the world of war, are shown to have only shallow foundations when tested in the subtler world of peace.

- Antonio is expressing the typical Elizabethan view of how daughters should obey their fathers when he says, 'I trust you will be ruled by your father' (2.1 38).
- The nobles are fooled by appearances but the low-born 'fools' of the Watch discover what lies beneath the surface.
- Claudio's conduct in rejecting Hero would have been more understandable by an Elizabethan audience because although men (like Benedick) could boast of their sexual conquests, 'honour' hypocritically demanded that a man's future wife should be chaste. Her 'value' as a bride (and Claudio was in his own word out to 'negotiate' his marriage) depended on her virginity. Nevertheless, by the time he shames her in church the audience already knows that she is innocent, and therefore that his vicious shaming is totally unjustified.
- Marriage is presented as the culmination of the play, and the only available option for women, but not as inevitably trouble-free. Many might question whether credulous, spiteful Claudio deserves Hero, and Benedick's final reference to cuckoldry suggests that problems are inevitable: 'there is no staff more reverend than one tipped with horn' (5.4 115). (A cuckold is a man whose wife has been unfaithful, and was often said in ridicule to grow horns on his head.)

Shakespeare's stance towards Elizabethan attitudes is not always critical: he was a man of his time and it jars on modern ears that there are remarks about race and colour that go unchallenged, notably Benedick's 'If I do not love her I am a Jew' (2.3 212) and Claudio's promise to marry the unseen maiden 'were she an Ethiop' (5.4 38).

The context of Messina

As in Shakespeare's main source, a tale by Bandello, *Much Ado About Nothing* is set in a Messina which sounds exotically far away, but it feels very much like Elizabethan England. Historically Messina, a Sicilian city, was ruled by Spain's House of Aragon – hence the fact that whilst Don Pedro is Spanish the other characters are Italian. Although military conflict is mentioned in the opening scene, Messina is a place far away from war. The focus is on living and loving rather than on fighting for your life.

The activities mentioned in the play are very much those that would be found in Elizabethan England – archery, angling, bear-baiting, falconry and pleasure in dining and drinking. As noted previously, nowhere but in Elizabethan England would a Watch like this one be found.

Messina is more a name rather than a real place, but it has characteristics that Shakespeare's audience would have recognised: it is a patriarchy where daughters like Hero are expected to do as their fathers tell them. Leonato is typical of England's developing merchant class – rich, but

Would the two princes lie, and Claudio lie?
(Leonato, 4.1 145)

not noble, and his deference towards the Prince is very evident. He is ambitious to become one of the aristocracy and is pleased when Count Claudio seeks the hand of his daughter. He cannot conceive of someone of the Prince's rank lying in his accusation of Hero. The Messina of the play is a man's world. This gives added edge to the portrayal of Beatrice as an unconventionally independent-minded woman, ready to challenge men and their assumptions of superiority. She establishes her credentials with the audience in the opening scene where she confuses and confounds the messenger.

The literary context

What Shakespeare wrote reflects the world in which he lived and the books he had read. To achieve the highest grades it is important to draw on the literary context for *Much Ado About Nothing* as well as on the more obvious historical context. That context includes Shakespeare's sources as well as ideas from the literature of his and earlier times.

The Elizabethan period was a time of unprecedented development in terms of literature and language. Theatres were flourishing – contemporary playwrights whose plays are still performed today included Christopher Marlowe and Ben Jonson among others – and poetry was very much in vogue. Shakespeare's own sonnet sequence was one of many, albeit a remarkable one, so Benedick who 'was not born under a rhyming planet' (5.2 30) provides an amusing contrast with his creator.

Shakespeare's sources

Romances in verse and prose, often translated from French or Italian, were also popular. One of those, a novella by the Italian writer Matteo Bandello, with its story of a chaste but slandered lady, was the main source for *Much Ado About Nothing*. Readers of romances expected exotic settings, sensational events and highly-wrought emotions – not bad as a description *Much Ado About Nothing*.

Build critical skills

Which characters has Shakespeare added to *Much Ado About Nothing* that were not in his sources? What difference do they make?

What audiences have seen as the real core of the play – the relationship between Beatrice and Benedick – was purely Shakespeare's invention. Without them the play would have been mere melodrama: exciting perhaps, but without much power to move an audience. Once Beatrice and Benedick are included, so much more is possible in terms of humour, social comment and genuine affection between individuals who are not just flies in society's web.

Courtly love

Courtly love, in which the beloved is adored but (usually) unattainable, was a central idea in medieval times and this carried through into Elizabethan literature: women tended either to be worshipped as goddesses or despised as whores. Claudio manages to move from one view of Hero to the other, and back again, with remarkable rapidity. However the love of Beatrice and Benedick offers a contrasting image of love, and we realise that Shakespeare was challenging the established images of courtly love rather than conforming to them.

Comedy

We do not have the same expectations of a comedy that Shakespeare's audience would have had because comedy as a genre term has shifted in its meaning. Comedies were distinguished from tragedies or history plays, and for Elizabethans to call a play a comedy meant that it had a happy ending, despite difficulties, rather than that it was 'funny' throughout. *Much Ado About Nothing* complies with the convention that comedies include:

- verbal humour
- young lovers facing but finally overcoming challenges
- deception or mistaken identity
- stock characters and amusing low-life characters
- clever plot twists
- music and dance
- a final resolution that features marriage as a happy ending

Classical allusions

Much Ado About Nothing, typically for Elizabethan writing, is full of classical allusions (i.e. references to Greek or Roman literature and myth). Shakespeare would have met the works of classical authors while attending grammar school in Stratford-on-Avon. He and his fellow poets and dramatists were familiar with Greek and Roman texts and therefore with classical images, ideas and stories. Among the classical figures mentioned in the play are:

- Jove, the notoriously lusty King of the Gods in Roman mythology (5.4 43–51)
- Hercules, the great Greek strongman who excelled at feats of sexuality as well as of strength (2.1 191)
- Troilus, a Trojan Prince whose lover Cressida became a byword for unfaithfulness (5.2 24)

The references are mock-heroic in that the gulf between Don Pedro or Benedick and the image of mighty Jove or Hercules is intended to be amusing.

Key quotation

Benedick is the antidote to courtly love:

methinks she's too low for a high praise, too brown for a fair praise, and too little for a great praise (1.1 126)

The audience context, then and now

Then

At least two performances of *Much Ado About Nothing* were given at court in 1613, but Shakespeare's original audiences, probably at the Globe Theatre, saw the play in 1598. Elizabethan audiences varied greatly in experience and expectations. Some would have been familiar with classical literature while others would have been there to laugh at the clowning of Will Kempe, to enjoy the songs and to jig along with the dancing. From the earliest performances people tended to think of the play as being about Beatrice and Benedick rather than about Claudio and Hero.

In *Much Ado About Nothing* there was something for everyone. Shakespeare's audiences would have found the wordplay much funnier than most modern audiences because language changes over time have made many of the jokes less obvious. The play has elements of melodrama which would have been popular with Elizabethans: it is sensational with its exaggerated characters, heightened emotions and exciting events.

Shakespeare's original audience would have expected to see and enjoy recognising stock characters such as the villain (Don John), the quiet, innocent beauty (Hero), the naïve lover (Claudio), the irate father (Leonato) and the man who scorns love until he becomes a lover (Benedick). More unusual is Beatrice, who is a feisty female, full of wit and more than a match for any man in verbal combat.

Now

The play has often, and understandably, been played for laughs, but modern audiences tend to respond more to the ways in which *Much Ado About Nothing* is a critique of society rather than just something to laugh at. A modern audience, accustomed to gender equality, is bound to see Beatrice's challenges to male assumptions in a different way from an Elizabethan audience in a theatre where women were not allowed to perform on stage. Recent all-female casts for performances gave particular power and poignancy to the exploration of the role of women in society but such performances would not have been possible in Shakespeare's time. Modern audiences have very different attitudes to women's role in society so their reactions to Beatrice might well mean that their admiration for her is even greater, but they may have less sympathy for passive Hero or credulous, chauvinist Claudio.

▲ Benedick and Beatrice in a 2004 production at the Globe Theatre

Build critical skills

The actors playing Benedick and Beatrice in this photograph are both female. How does that change your reaction to them?

REVIEW YOUR LEARNING

(Answers are given on p. 102.)

1 Write your own explanation of what you think examiners mean by 'context'.

2 What did Shakespeare's usual theatre (the Globe) look like?

3 How might the layout of the theatre have influenced audience reactions?

4 Which main characters were not in Shakespeare's sources?

5 Give an example of how knowledge of Shakespeare's sources has informed your understanding.

6 How does it influence your response to know that Leonato's assumptions about Hero's obedience would have been typical of his time?

7 Select three quotations that are illuminated by your awareness of Shakespeare's time.

8 How does *Much Ado About Nothing* conform to the Elizabethan conventions of the comedy genre?

9 Give an example of the possible impact on a modern audience of the changes in language since Shakespeare's time.

10 How might the attitudes of modern audiences differ from those of an Elizabethan audience?

GRADE *FOCUS*

Grade 5
To achieve Grade 5, students will show a clear understanding of the context in which the play was written.

Grade 8
To achieve Grade 8, students will make perceptive, critical comments about the ways that contextual factors affect the choices that the playwright makes. They also need to analyse how different Elizabethan and modern audiences might respond in different ways to the play and to particular productions.

Plot and structure

Target your thinking

- What are the main events of the play? (**AO1**)
- How do these events unfold, act by act? (**AO1, AO2**)
- How does Shakespeare use structure in presenting the play? (**AO2**)

Plot

Act 1

- The Prince of Aragon, Don Pedro, returns to Messina with Claudio and Benedick, to be welcomed by Leonato.
- Leonato's niece Beatrice and Benedick resume their war of words.
- Claudio declares his love for Leonato's daughter Hero and is mocked by Benedick, a professed bachelor.
- The Prince offers to woo Hero on Claudio's behalf.
- The Prince's brother, Don John, declares himself a malcontent (villain) and seeks to spite his brother by spoiling Claudio's intended marriage.

In the opening scene Shakespeare sends signals to the audience about the main characters and the likely focus of the drama. We are told that the military conflict is over – the lightheartedness of the opening conversations signals that Messina is a context of peace in which the fighting is likely to be about love rather than war and verbal rather than physical. We hear briefly about Claudio's bravery but the emphasis (even before he appears) is on Beatrice's relationship with Benedick. When Claudio's admiration for Hero is mentioned we can guess that the play's focus will be on these four and how the contrasting pairs will finish up married. Given the menacing presence of Don John and the imagery which suggests that Claudio loves with his eyes rather than his heart, there is potential for tragedy through manipulation and misinterpretation.

Build critical skills

Does the scene on the opposite page reflect how you imagined the return of Don Pedro? How does it compare with the depiction of his return on page 8?

▲ The return of Don Pedro in a 2008 Globe Theatre production

The action is set in Messina, a distant, romantically 'foreign' city, at the home of Leonato, a rich nobleman. The recent war is over and the victorious Prince of Aragon, Don Pedro, is accompanied by the 'right noble' Claudio who has distinguished himself in the war. When he arrives he is welcomed by Leonato whose niece is Beatrice, a witty and voluble young woman, who fires verbal volleys at Benedick, one of the returning soldiers, before he even appears. Leonato explains that Beatrice and Benedick enjoy their 'duel of wit'. We witness this as soon as they speak to each other: Beatrice comments acidly, 'I wonder that you will still be talking, Signor Benedick, nobody marks you' (1.1 86).

This couple are more mature, witty and intelligent than Hero and Claudio. We assume from their first exchange that Beatrice and Benedick will be verbal antagonists but also that (in accordance with the traditions of Elizabethan comedy) they may well end up married to each other.

The Prince's bastard brother, Don John, who was the enemy in the recent conflict, is now supposedly reconciled with his brother. He is the stereotypical villain and Shakespeare's audience would have recognised him as such. His terse replies simmer with resentment and suggest future trouble.

Claudio is enamoured of Leonato's daughter Hero, but mainly because of her looks: 'she is the sweetest lady that ever I looked on'. Don Pedro offers to woo Hero on Claudio's behalf. Benedick mocks Claudio's infatuation with Hero, declaring himself a 'professed tyrant' to women and that he will never marry. Claudio's first questions about Hero are not romantic: they are whether she is an only child (and therefore would

Build critical skills

What impression of Beatrice's attitude to Benedick is given by her questions below?

I pray you, how many hath he killed and eaten in these wars? But how many hath he killed? – for indeed I promised to eat all of his killing.

(1.1 31–33)

Build critical skills

How does Shakespeare use animal imagery here to present the relationship between Beatrice and Benedick?

BENEDICK

Well, you are a rare parrot-teacher.

BEATRICE

A bird of my tongue is better than a beast of yours.

BENEDICK

I would my horse had the speed of your tongue, and so good a continuer: but keep your way a God's name. I have done.

BEATRICE

You always end with a jade's trick: I know you of old.

(1.1 103–107)

Key quotations

There is a kind of merry war betwixt Signor Benedick and her.
(Leonato, 1.1 45–46)

Benedick declares there will never be

Benedick the married man
(1.1 199)

I cannot hide what I am.

I am a plain-dealing villain.
(Don John, 1.3 10 and 1.3 23)

inherit Leonato's fortune) and 'Is she not a modest young lady?' Hero's virginity will later become the centre of Claudio's concern and of the most dramatic moments of the play. Antonio, Leonato's brother, has been told by a servant of the Prince's intention to woo Hero at the masked ball. He informs Leonato, but neither brother realises that the Prince's wooing will be for Claudio, not for himself. Leonato's assumption that Hero will automatically accept the Prince's proposal is an indicator of a woman's (especially a daughter's) subservient role in male-dominated Messina. Because, unlike Hero, she does not fit this female stereotype, independent-minded Beatrice is immediately more appealing to a modern audience.

Don John's servant Borachio has overheard the Prince's plan to woo Hero for Claudio. Don John resents 'the exquisite Claudio' for having helped to defeat him. He sees Claudio's intention to marry Hero as a 'model to build mischief on' and sneeringly describes Hero as 'a very forward March-chick'. His servants Conrade and Borachio declare their allegiance to him.

Act 2

- Leonato talks about marriage with Hero and Beatrice. He fears that Beatrice is too outspoken.
- At a masked ball Don Pedro woos Hero and Beatrice insults Benedick, pretending not to recognise him.
- Don John tells the disguised Claudio that the Prince is wooing Hero for himself.
- Benedick offers mock sympathy to Claudio, but avoids Beatrice.
- Claudio is depressed until eventually the Prince admits that he has won Hero's hand on behalf of Claudio. Claudio is overjoyed but lost for words.
- The Prince suggests that trying to bring together Benedick and Beatrice would fill the time enjoyably up to the wedding of Claudio and Hero.
- Don John's servant, Borachio, suggests a plot to deceive Claudio into believing that Hero is unfaithful.
- Benedick affirms his intention to stay single, but changes his mind when he overhears Leonato, the Prince and Claudio discussing how much Beatrice loves him. The transformation from anti-lover to lover is immediate.

Beatrice's wit and independence of mind are evident in her conversation with her uncles Leonato and Antonio. Being a conventional figure, Leonato shares his fears with Beatrice that, 'thou wilt never get thee a husband if thou be so shrewd of thy tongue'. His daughter Hero, by contrast, is ready to be ruled by her father over whom she should marry. Beatrice makes fun of Hero's obedience, suggesting that she should be ready to decline an unsuitable suitor by saying 'father, as it please me.'

She denies that she herself will ever be 'fitted with a husband' as Leonato hopes.

Build critical skills

How does Shakespeare use the extract below to present the contrast between Beatrice and Hero?

Yes faith, it is my cousin's duty to make curtsy, and say, father, as it please you: but yet for all that, cousin, let him be a handsome fellow, or else make another curtsy, and say, father, as it please me.

(Beatrice, 2.1 39–41)

During a masked ball at Leonato's the women make fun of the masked males, knowing full well who they are. The masked-but-recognisable Prince woos Hero, and Beatrice, claiming that she does not recognise him, insults (disguised) Benedick as 'the Prince's jester, a very dull fool'. Don John, pretending that he thinks Claudio is Benedick, tells Claudio that the Prince is wooing Hero for himself, and Claudio believes him.

Benedick describes Claudio as 'poor hurt fowl' because he thinks that the Prince has stolen Hero, but is smarting himself from Beatrice's comments which he attributes to her 'base, though bitter, disposition.' He tells the Prince that 'she misused me past the endurance of a block!' When Beatrice approaches, Benedick leaves because 'I cannot endure my Lady Tongue'.

Beatrice arrives with Claudio who, still thinking that the Prince has stolen his love, is described as 'civil, count, civil as an orange, and something of that jealous complexion'. This image of an orange will be used again later, with vicious power. We learn that Beatrice and Benedick were once close, and that Beatrice feels Benedick won her heart 'with false dice'.

After some gentle teasing the Prince reveals that he has won Hero's hand on Claudio's behalf. Claudio is suitably tongue-tied. He says, 'Silence is the perfectest herald of joy' and then, 'Lady, as you are mine, I am yours'. Claudio's tongue-tied response to the offer of Hero reminds us how eloquent Beatrice and Benedick are. The sophisticated older couple contrast with the youthful and naïve Claudio and Hero. Beatrice suggests that Hero should speak or 'stop his mouth with a kiss' a phrase that will be used again later, but by Benedick about Beatrice. Beatrice's mocking comments about needing to cry 'Heigh-ho for a husband' prompt the Prince to make a lighthearted offer of himself, which Beatrice charmingly declines. The Prince later observes that 'She cannot bear to hear tell of a husband', and thinks 'She were an excellent wife for Benedick' since he feels that 'Benedick is not the unhopefullest husband that I know'. The comic sub-plot is clearly established when the Prince declares that he will 'bring Signor Benedick and Lady Beatrice into a mountain of affection,

Build critical skills

Which of Claudio's words plant questions in the mind of the audience about the quality of his love for Hero?

Let every eye negotiate for itself,

And trust no agent: for beauty is a witch

(Claudio, 2.1 134–135)

Build critical skills

What image of the relationship between Benedick and Beatrice is created by Shakespeare's choice of imagery here?

I stood like a man at a mark, with a whole army shooting at me: she speaks poniards, and every word stabs

(Benedick: 2.1 186–187)

How does Shakespeare's wording of Borachio's plan relate to the theme of differences between appearance and reality?

I will so fashion the matter that Hero shall be absent,—and there shall appear such seeming truth of Hero's disloyalty that jealousy shall be called assurance and all the preparation overthrown.

(Borachio, 2.2 35–37)

What might Shakespeare's audience have anticipated as a result of these words of Benedick's?

I do much wonder, that one man seeing how much another man is a fool, when he dedicates his behaviours to love, will, after he hath laughed at such shallow follies in others, become the argument of his own scorn, by falling in love: and such a man is Claudio.

(2.3 7–10)

th'one with th'other' (2.1 275–277). The plan to bring Beatrice and Benedick together is dramatically important – without it the play would have been much more serious and could have become a tragedy.

Don John's first attempt to create discord has failed. However Borachio tells Don John that his friendship with Margaret, Hero's serving-maid, will enable him to deceive Claudio and the Prince into believing that Hero has been unfaithful: not a virgin but 'a contaminated stale'. He will make it appear as if Hero is meeting another man in her bedchamber, when in fact it will be Margaret. Borachio claims his deceit will provide 'Proof enough, to misuse the prince, to vex Claudio, to undo Hero, and kill Leonato'. Appearance is again a central issue. Borachio intends to manipulate appearances to create a 'seeming truth', which the audience knows to be false but which will be a moral challenge for Claudio and the Prince. Once he understands the potential for mischief, Don John is pleased enough with the prospect of wrecking Claudio's marriage to promise a thousand ducats to Borachio as his fee.

Benedick soliloquises (thinks aloud to the audience) about how foolish men are when in love. He affirms his determination not to 'become the argument of his own scorn by falling in love' but then hides in an arbour when the Prince and other men arrive. Shakespeare has an interlude of song, which includes the line 'men are deceivers ever' and there are puns about noting and notes.

Benedick overhears the Prince, Claudio and Leonato talking of Beatrice's love for him. Leonato says that it is 'most wonderful, that she should so dote on Signor Benedick, whom she hath in all outward behaviours seemed ever to abhor' (2.3 85–87). The Prince adds that Benedick 'hath a contemptible spirit' and is 'unworthy so good a lady'.

▲ What makes Benedick believe what he hears when hidden in the arbour?

There is comment on whether Beatrice's antagonism towards Benedick is 'counterfeit' and whether she is 'exceeding wise' in 'everything but in loving Benedick.' They claim that they need to protect Beatrice from Benedick's 'contemptible [i.e. disdainful] spirit' and therefore will not tell him of her love for him. The impact is immediate – Benedick says, 'This can be no trick' but the audience knows that it is precisely that, and having rejected the idea that this could be a 'gull' because 'the white-bearded fellow speaks it', Benedick declares that he will be 'horribly in love with her'. Ruefully he acknowledges that 'I may chance have some odd quirks and remnants of wit broken on me, because I have railed so long against marriage: but doth not the appetite alter?' and 'the world must be peopled'. From then on he (mis)interprets anything Beatrice says as evidence of her affection for him. When she is sent to call Benedick in to dinner she is met with a disconcertingly warm response.

Act 3

- Hero and her ladies deceive Beatrice into thinking that Benedick is in love with her.
- The Prince and Claudio mock Benedick but are then told by Don John that he can show them that Hero is unfaithful.
- The Watch are given the advice by Dogberry and Verges that they should carry out their duties with minimum effort. Despite this they overhear Borachio telling Conrade how he has deceived Claudio and the Prince, and they arrest the two villains.
- Hero is prepared for her wedding and Beatrice is teased for being in love.
- The Watch try to inform Leonato of the plot to defile Hero, but he is too busy with the wedding preparations to listen to Dogberry.

Hero and her ladies (speaking in verse, unlike the men who spoke and joked in prose) deceive Beatrice in her turn into thinking that Benedick is in love with her. Structurally this scene was needed to balance the 'gulling' of Benedick in the previous scene. It also allowed Shakespeare to show Hero as a more rounded personality, and will make her forthcoming shaming more painful in the eyes of the audience.

Hero says and does far more in this scene than previously: she is the fluently confident leader of the group. 'Look where Beatrice like a lapwing runs/Close by to the ground, to hear our conference'. She even says, 'I'll devise some honest slanders to stain my cousin with.' She adds, with an irony she is unaware of, that 'one doth not know/How much an ill word may empoison liking'.

Key quotations

Benedick says of Beatrice:

she speaks poniards, and every word stabs

and

I cannot endure my Lady Tongue (2.1 187 and 2.1 207)

He also comments:

When I said I would die a bachelor, I did not think I should live till I were married. (2.3 197–198)

Beatrice says Claudio is:

civil, count, civil as an orange, and something of that jealous complexion. (2.1 223)

The Prince comments: *Benedick is not the unhopefullest husband that I know* (2.1 285)

Build critical skills

What does this image suggest about Beatrice?

She's limed I warrant you; we have caught her, madam. (Ursula, 3.1 104)

Hero's disparaging description of Beatrice, intended to shame her into caring for Benedick, is quite hurtful:

> nature never framed a woman's heart
> Of prouder stuff than that of Beatrice:
> Disdain and scorn ride sparkling in her eyes
> Misprising what they look on.

(3.1 49–52)

Beatrice emerges from her hiding place a changed woman, ready to reciprocate Benedick's supposed affection: 'I will requite thee,/Taming my wild heart to thy loving hand.'

▲ Beatrice (hiding), with Hero and Ursula

Build critical skills

How serious is Don Pedro when he says this of Benedick? How far do you agree with his description?

from the crown of his head to the sole of his foot, he is all mirth

(3.2 6–7)

The Prince and Claudio make fun of Benedick for seeming to be in love. Don Pedro says 'there's no true drop of blood in him to be truly touched with love: if he be sad, he wants money' (3.2 14–15). They praise his wit and merriment whilst observing his untypical melancholy and commenting that his beard has been shaved off.

Benedick leaves calling the Prince and Claudio 'hobby-horses' for mocking him. Then Don John enters and the mood changes abruptly: he disconcerts Claudio and the Prince by claiming that 'the lady is disloyal' and, crudely, that she is 'Leonato's Hero, your Hero, every man's Hero' (3.2 78). Don John claims he can prove that Hero is unfaithful: 'you shall see her chamber window entered even the night before her wedding day'.

Claudio's immediate reaction is violent and vicious – he will shame her rather than marry her. The Prince agrees to join in the public disgrace of Hero, both seeming more than ready to believe that Hero is guilty.

The play's mood, which was darkening rapidly, changes again with the introduction of Dogberry, the constable of the Watch, and his partner Verges. When Dogberry and Verges enter with their fractured phrases the audience is alerted to their verbal humour which is the opposite of witty and almost a parody of the verbal dexterity elsewhere. Words often mean one thing to Dogberry or Verges and the opposite to the audience: almost immediately the idea of having to 'suffer salvation' or be punished for 'allegiance' signals that sense and nonsense will be inextricably and amusingly entwined. Dogberry's incompetence is majestic – he neither speaks nor acts sensibly in choosing people to be the Watch and in advising them how to avoid trouble rather than to arrest villains. He says that neighbour Seacoal is, 'the most senseless and fit man for the constable of the watch.'

The one piece of good guidance that Dogberry gives is vital to the play – to 'watch about Signor Leonato's door'. It is deeply ironic that, despite their misunderstandings, it is the Watch (not the nobles) who discover the plan to disgrace Hero. They overhear Borachio and Conrade talking drunkenly about the superficiality of fashion, and misinterpret what is said enough to think there is a thief called 'Deformed'. However when Borachio goes on to tell Conrade how Hero will be shamed in church, the watch do their duty and arrest them. Somewhat surprisingly (but they are drunk) Borachio and Conrade allow themselves to be arrested.

Act 3 scene 4 focuses on women and their feelings. Hero is being prepared for her wedding but says, 'my heart is exceeding heavy'. The talk is again of clothes and fashion and Margaret seems oblivious to any trouble that her meeting with Borachio the night before might cause, since she jokes at the expense of Hero and Beatrice. Beatrice is feeling sick so Margaret mockingly recommends 'distilled *Carduus benedictus*'. Having commented that Benedick too is changed, she says to Beatrice, 'methinks you look with your eyes as other women do.' That is just what the men, Claudio and the Prince, have done.

Dogberry and Verges meet Leonato at what he says is 'a busy time'. They try, in their wonderfully long-winded way, to tell Leonato of the knavery that they have discovered, but Dogberry seems equally eager to patronise the 'good old man' Verges. They are, as Leonato says in exasperation, 'tedious' and he is too busy hastening to his daughter's marriage to listen to their explanations. He leaves them to examine the malefactors without him, which leaves the audience in a state of increasing uncertainty about what will happen: whether the plot will be revealed in time or Hero will be shamed in the church.

Build critical skills

What is the impact on the audience of Claudio's reaction to Don John's claim that Hero is false?

tomorrow in the congregation, where I should wed, there will I shame her.

(Claudio, 3.2 90–91)

Build critical skills

What impression of the Watch does Shakespeare create through words such as these?

the most peaceable way for you, if you do take a thief, is, to let him show himself what he is, and steal out of your company.

(3.3 4–50)

Key quotations

tomorrow in the congregation, where I should wed, there will I shame her.
(Claudio, 3.2 91–92)

you shall comprehend all vagrom men.
(Dogberry, 3.3 21–22)

our watch, sir, have indeed comprehended two aspitious persons, and we would have them this morning examined before your worship.

(Dogberry, 3.5 35–37)

What are the dramatic effects of Leonato's decision to leave examining Conrade and Borachio to Dogberry and the Watch?

Act 4

- At the wedding ceremony Claudio refuses to marry Hero and shames her in public, backed up by the Prince.
- Leonato also accuses Hero, who faints helplessly.
- Beatrice and the Friar believe in Hero's innocence, and suspect Don John. The Friar suggests pretending that Hero is dead to find out the truth.
- Beatrice and Benedick admit their love for each other, but Beatrice demands as proof of his affection that he challenges Claudio to a duel.
- Despite Dogberry's hilariously inappropriate attempt to question Borachio, the Sexton does find out the truth.

This is a pivotal point in the play. The mood here still has potential for tragedy since Don John's plot has been discovered but not fully revealed. The wedding scene begins with misunderstandings: the Friar asks Claudio if he has come 'to marry this lady' and when Claudio replies 'No' Leonato assumes that he is quibbling over language rather than stating that he will not marry her. When Leonato claims that he dare make Claudio's answer for him, Claudio snarls 'Oh what men dare do!' and pretends to take Hero in marriage, before returning her to her father, saying 'Give not this rotten orange to your friend' and accusing her of being 'an approved wanton'. When bewildered Hero asks Claudio if she ever 'seemed' otherwise than virtuous to him, Claudio rages against 'seeming': 'Out on thee seeming, I will write against it!' and accuses Hero of 'savage sensuality'. The Prince supports Claudio, claiming that he too saw her 'Talk with a ruffian at her chamber window'. Benedick, whose style is usually one of lengthy exaggeration, offers only the brief understatement, 'This looks not like a nuptial.' Again everything depends on how appearances are interpreted – this focus on seeming reminds the audience that in Messina there is usually a gulf between appearance and reality.

Hero stands helpless against the battery of male accusations:

Oh God defend me, how am I beset!

What kind of catechising call you this?

(4.1 71–72)

When her protestations of innocence are dismissed by Don Pedro and Don John as well as by Claudio, Hero collapses and Claudio, Don John and Don Pedro leave. The action is based around the male characters' assumption that what they think has to be the truth, but the audience knows it to be a deception and Hero, as a female, is helpless.

▲ Hero collapses under accusation

Beatrice comes to Hero's aid, but Leonato's first reaction is to hope that Hero has died to escape the shame. Leonato, concerned only about himself rather than his daughter, laments ever having had a child.

Hero was presented as a pawn earlier in the play – to be allied to the Prince or to Claudio as her father deemed fit. In the church she is shown to be helpless against the barrage of male accusations of unfaithfulness. Weakness (i.e. fainting) is her only weapon and, despite Beatrice's qualities, as a woman she is unable to avenge her cousin – in the male-dominated world of Messina she has to rely on Benedick to be her warrior. Benedick is untypically speechless: 'I am so attired in wonder, I know not what to say.' Beatrice however has no doubts: 'Oh on my soul my cousin is belied!'

The Friar, who has been 'noting' Hero, says there has been 'some biting error' and that 'There is some strange misprision in the princes'. Benedick identifies 'John the bastard' as the likely source of villainy. Leonato is now undecided: if Hero is guilty he will kill her, and if not, 'The proudest of them shall well hear of it'. Following the Friar's suggestions it is decided that Hero should 'die to live' through feigning her death until her innocence is revealed: 'The supposition of the lady's death/Will quench the wonder of her infamy.' It is not unusual in Shakespeare for a Friar to

Build critical skills

What is the dramatic impact of Shakespeare having her father denounce Hero at this point in the play?

doth not every earthly thing

Cry shame upon her?

(Leonato, 4.1 113–114)

Key quotations

*Oh what men dare do!
What men may do!
What men daily do,
not knowing what they
do!*
(Claudio, 4.1 14–15)

*Oh what authority and
show of truth*

*Can cunning sin cover
itself withal!*
(Claudio, 4.1 30–31)

*I do love nothing in the
world so well as you, is
not that strange?*
(Benedick, 4.1 259–260)

my cousin is belied!
(Beatrice, 4.1 139)

Build critical skills

What gives
Claudio's use of this
image its dramatic
power?

*Give not this rotten
orange to your friend.*
(4.1 27)

be the one who proposes a way out of a difficulty: the same happens in *Romeo and Juliet*, for example. Here the deception over Hero's death is intended to reveal the truth of Claudio's feelings, even though the Friar does not yet know about Don John's use of deception to hide the truth.

Only Beatrice and Benedick remain on stage and their mutual love emerges in their belief in Hero's faithfulness. Benedick says, 'I do love nothing in the world so well as you, is not that strange?' When Benedick says, 'bid me do anything for thee', Beatrice's chilling reply is 'Kill Claudio.' Beatrice is furious that since she is a woman she cannot physically avenge her cousin: 'I cannot be a man with wishing, therefore I will die a woman with grieving.' Benedick checks that Beatrice really does believe in Hero's innocence and then agrees to challenge Claudio.

Act 5

- Leonato laments the suffering that his daughter's disgrace has brought him.
- Leonato and Antonio, increasingly convinced of Hero's innocence, offer challenges to Claudio and Don Pedro.
- Benedick challenges Claudio to a duel.
- The deception practised on Claudio and the Prince is revealed.
- Repentant Claudio agrees to marry Leonato's niece in penance.
- Beatrice and Benedick talk about their love for each other.
- Claudio and the Prince hold a vigil for Hero.
- Claudio is married to a masked lady who is revealed as Hero.
- Beatrice consents to marry Benedick.
- Don John, who fled from Messina, has been caught.

Leonato laments at length on his (not his daughter's) situation, saying that he will take counsel from no-one who has not suffered as he has: 'let no comforter delight mine ear/But such a one whose wrongs do suit with mine.'

Leonato now feels increasingly convinced that Hero was wronged and when Claudio and the Prince appear, unrepentant, Leonato calls Claudio a 'dissembler'. Leonato and Antonio, although old men, are ready to fight with the Prince and Claudio. Antonio is fierce about, 'Scambling, out-facing, fashion-monging boys,/That lie, and cog, and flout, deprave and slander,/Go anticly, show outward hideousness.' The Prince and Claudio, still convinced of Hero's guilt, will not listen to them.

Benedick appears and maintains a dignified distance whilst Claudio and the Prince seek to jest with him – he says his wit is in his scabbard rather than his mouth. Benedick then quietly issues a challenge to Claudio saying, 'You have killed a sweet lady, and her death shall fall heavy on you.' At first Claudio and the Prince do not think Benedick is serious, but before leaving he tells them that John the Bastard is fled, and they realise that 'he is in earnest'.

The Watch arrive but Dogberry's explanations of the crime are 'too cunning to be understood.' The villains finally confess to their deceit, to the horror of the Prince and of Claudio who says, 'I have drunk poison whiles he uttered it'. Claudio feels (suspiciously quickly?) that Hero's image 'doth appear in the rare semblance that I loved it first'. Leonato thanks them witheringly for his daughter's death. To atone for his 'mistaking' Claudio agrees immediately with the request that he marry the daughter of Leonato's brother. Dogberry departs, rewarded financially but in typical verbal confusion. Claudio and the penitent Prince leave to mount an all-night vigil at Hero's tomb.

Benedick practises the art of writing as a lover with the help of Margaret. Beatrice enters and after their traditional verbal jousting Benedick says, 'But I must tell thee plainly, Claudio undergoes my challenge.' They discuss how they 'suffer love' for each other and are then told by Ursula that Don John's plot has been revealed. The two plots (Hero and Claudio, Beatrice and Benedick) come together at this point in the play as Benedick's allegiance proves to be to Beatrice rather than to Claudio.

Claudio and the Prince grieve for Hero as dawn breaks. They then leave with Claudio intending to marry Antonio's daughter. Claudio's act of dawn penance is symbolically significant: the darkness in the play is giving way to light and the audience can feel that justice has been done. Benedick asks the Friar to marry him to Beatrice and is puzzled by Leonato's comments about the 'eye of love' with which he sees Beatrice and she sees him ('Your answer, sir, is enigmatical'). Don Pedro notes that Benedick has a 'February face' which reflects his ambivalence about the 'state of honourable marriage'.

Here Shakespeare has Leonato introduce yet another twist to the theme of appearance and reality with the suggestion that Claudio should marry his niece, the disguised Hero. Claudio is married to a masked lady who proves to be Hero and says, 'One Hero died defiled, but I do live.'

Beatrice too is finally unmasked but says that she loves Benedick 'no more than reason', a sentiment that Benedick echoes. Beatrice eventually consents to marriage 'upon great persuasion, and partly to save your life'. This enables the Prince to say, 'How dost thou, Benedick the married man?' and Benedick to respond, 'Get thee a wife.'

We hear in the final lines that Don John has been caught.

Build critical skills

How does Borachio's comment relate to the theme of appearance and reality?

What your wisdoms could not discover, these shallow fools have brought to light.

(5.1 205)

Key quotations

I have deceived even your very eyes.
(Borachio, 5.1 204)

Runs not this speech like iron through your blood?
(Don Pedro, 5.1 214)

I thank you, Princes, for my daughter's death.
(Leonato, 5.1 235)

Yet sinned I not but in mistaking.
(Claudio, 5.1 241)

such a February face
(Don Pedro [of Benedick], 5.4 41)

How dost thou, Benedick the married man?
(Don Pedro, 5.4 97)

One Hero died defiled, but I do live
(Hero, 5.4 63)

since I do purpose to marry, I will think nothing to any purpose that the world can say against it.
(Benedick, 5.4 101–102)

The play's structure

Remember that you will gain higher marks in the GCSE examination if you can write about structure as well as about content and character.

The play has two interrelated plots:

1 The conspiracy by Don John to disgrace Hero and prevent her marriage to Claudio.

2 The union of Beatrice and Benedick despite their alleged dislike of each other and of marriage.

The play has elements of tragedy and comedy: because Shakespeare combines the two structurally through the double plot, the tragic and comic elements are linked in such a way that the audience keeps both in mind. When we hear Claudio's savage denunciation of Hero's infidelity we already know that Borachio's deception has been discovered, which reduces the tragic tension, yet the revelation of the evil depends on 'tedious' Dogberry, which (in a comic way) heightens the tension in case the truth is not communicated in time.

It is not as simple as saying that the main plot is tragic and the sub-plot is comic: Dogberry and Verges are comic characters yet are part of the main plot. There are moments that are fraught with tragic potential, but they are preceded or followed by moments of witty amusement through Beatrice and Benedick or moments of laugh-out-loud comedy with Dogberry and Verges.

MAIN PLOT (Hero and Claudio)	SUB-PLOT (Beatrice and Benedick)
1.1 Claudio and the Prince return to Messina. Claudio declares his love for Hero.	1.1 Beatrice meets Benedick again and their verbal warfare continues. Benedick mocks love and Claudio, declaring his intention to stay single.
1.2 Leonato wrongly believes that the Prince will woo Hero for himself.	
1.3 Don John's first plot, to dismay Claudio, is hatched but based on a mistaken overhearing.	
2.1 The masked ball: the Prince woos Hero on Claudio's behalf and then hands her over to Claudio.	2.1 Beatrice declares her intention to stay single. At the masked ball Beatrice insults disguised Benedick. The plan to bring Beatrice and Benedick together is made.
2.2 Don John's second plot is formed when Borachio suggests the deceit.	
	2.3 Benedick is 'gulled' into thinking that Beatrice loves him.

MAIN PLOT (Hero and Claudio)	SUB-PLOT (Beatrice and Benedick)
	3.1 Beatrice is 'gulled' into thinking that Benedick loves her.
3.2 Don John says that he can show Claudio and the Prince evidence of Hero's infidelity.	
3.3 Dogberry recruits and instructs the Watch.	
3.4 Hero is prepared for the wedding.	3.4 Beatrice is teased over being in love.
3.5 Dogberry tries to tell Leonato of the plot, but Leonato is too busy to listen.	
4.1 Claudio shames Hero in church and she faints. The Friar suggests pretending that she has died.	4.1 Benedick sides with Beatrice in believing that Hero has been wronged. He agrees to challenge Claudio.
4.2 Despite the lack of clarity in Dogberry's questioning, the truth of the deception is revealed.	
5.1 Leonato and Antonio challenge Claudio and the Prince. The truth is revealed to Claudio and the Prince. Penitent Claudio agrees to marry Leonato's niece.	5.1 Benedick, unaware of Borachio's deception, offers a real challenge to Claudio, confirming his love for Beatrice.
5.2 The truth of Hero's innocence is made public.	5.2 Benedick writes a poem to Beatrice.
5.3 Claudio keeps a vigil for Hero.	
5.4 Claudio finds that his bride is Hero after all.	5.4 Benedick asks the Friar to marry him to Beatrice. She agrees 'upon great persuasion'.

GRADE *FOCUS*

Grade 5
To achieve Grade 5, students will show a clear and detailed understanding of the whole play and of the effects created by its structure.

Grade 8
To achieve Grade 8, students' responses will display a comprehensive understanding of explicit and implicit meanings in the play as a whole and will examine and evaluate Shakespeare's use of structure in detail.

GRADE *BOOSTER*

Usually, the examination question will explain briefly where in the play the extract is taken from. It won't necessarily tell you what happens just before or just after the extract, but when writing about plot and structure, it can be helpful to know. For example, you may be able to refer to the use of contrast with other events, or dramatic irony. So make sure you have a really clear grasp of the order of events.

REVIEW YOUR LEARNING

(Answers are given on p. 102.)

1 How does Shakespeare tell the audience that Beatrice and Benedick are likely to end up married?

2 What characteristics do Beatrice and Benedick have in common that distinguish them from the other characters?

3 How does Shakespeare create the contrast between Hero and Beatrice?

4 What do you think an audience might find most amusing about the scene in the arbour when Benedick overhears that Beatrice is in love with him?

5 What characterises the words that Shakespeare gives to Dogberry?

6 What image do you associate with Claudio?

7 Why does Don John behave as he does?

8 What is the dramatic impact of having the Watch discover the villainy rather than the nobles?

9 Do you think that Claudio deserves to marry Hero?

10 How far do you agree that Beatrice and Benedick, rather than Hero and Claudio, are the more significant couple for an audience?

Characterisation

Target your thinking

- How does Shakespeare present the main characters? (**AO2**)
- What is distinctive about each character's language and actions? (**AO1, AO2**)
- What do the different characters contribute to the play? (**AO1 AO2**)

When writing about characters always bear in mind that they are not real people – they were created by Shakespeare to fulfil his dramatic purposes. For example, Beatrice and Benedick did not exist in Shakespeare's sources, but he felt it necessary to invent them, along with Dogberry and Verges.

Characters in the play

Beatrice

From her first comments about 'Signor Mountanto' (1.1 23) Shakespeare presents Beatrice as intelligently witty, confidently voluble and extremely interested in Benedick. He is the continual focus of her words and feelings and the target for her barbed comments. In the very first scene Shakespeare has her say to Benedick, 'I know you of old', and there are times when we wonder if her antagonism is a cover for unrequited affection, tinged with bitterness. At one point Benedick says, 'it is the base, though bitter, disposition of Beatrice, that puts the world into her person, and so gives me out' (2.1 157).

Beatrice has no father trying to command or control her: she is an independent-minded woman in the male-dominated world of Messina. Shakespeare makes her a deliberate contrast with Hero so that her qualities are more apparent. Beatrice gently (and unconventionally) chides Hero over being so submissive in the choice of her husband, suggesting that rather than say, 'Father, as it please you' she should say, 'Father, as it please me' (2.1 39–41). We enjoy and admire Beatrice's wit and spirit, but since her determination not to marry 'till God make men of some other metal than earth' matches Benedick's determination to stay single, we guess that she too will finally be married. Shakespeare makes the vehemence of her tirades against men so extreme that it invites an audience to expect her to change: 'Would it not grieve a woman to be overmastered with a piece of valiant dust? To make an account of her life to a clod of wayward marl?' (2.1 43–45). At times her conversation

Key quotations

Beatrice:

I wonder that you will still be talking, Signor Benedick, nobody marks you.
(1.1.86)

I had rather hear my dog bark at a crow than a man swear he loves me.
(1.1.97)

Oh on my soul, my cousin is belied!
(4.1.139)

Kill Claudio.
(4.1.279)

is explicitly sexual: when the Prince says of Benedick 'You have put him down lady' (2.1 214) she replies, naughtily, 'So I would not he should do me, my lord.'

Shakespeare presents Beatrice as a good and loyal friend: she is the first to declare her belief in Hero's innocence and is both furious and frustrated at the impossibility of a woman challenging Claudio: 'Oh God that I were a man! I would eat his heart in the market place' (4.1 294). The fierceness of that claim is matched by her demand that if Benedick wishes to prove his love for her he should kill Claudio.

Beatrice and Benedick marry on their own terms, not society's, and her final acceptance of Benedick is anything but conventionally submissive: 'I yield upon great persuasion, and partly to save your life, for I was told, you were in a consumption' (5.4 94).

Hero

Shakespeare created Hero and Beatrice as the contrasting female characters within the quartet of lovers: one conventional, quiet and submissive, the other wittily unconventional. This makes Hero a much less appealing character than Beatrice on stage – she demurely accepts the decisions of her father about her life, and her response to Claudio's charge of infidelity is to faint rather than to fight back. When the truth of her innocence is revealed she accepts Claudio swiftly, almost silently and without any accusation; instead she re-affirms her virtue and switches her attention to Beatrice and Benedick. The only times when Hero does seem a more rounded character are when she is masked at the ball and has a witty exchange with Don Pedro, and when she is with her women, plotting to ensnare Beatrice. Then she even pretends that she will 'devise some honest slanders/To stain my cousin with' (3.1 84). It is significant that this is a moment when there are no men present and because Beatrice is hiding she does not offer a contrast. When she is in her daughter role she reverts to quiet submissiveness.

Hero, whose name was in Shakespeare's sources, was taken from Greek mythology. She was the archetypal innocent and beautiful young woman who could not live without her lover Leander. Because Shakespeare gave her a symbolic, sacrificial role we never see much depth to her character although she is often the focus of dramatic attention. Her outward appearance is what mattered to Claudio rather than her inner beauty: 'she is the sweetest lady that ever I looked on' (1.1 139).

The play's most powerful moment, one about which Hero had serious misgivings in advance ('my heart is exceeding heavy'; 3.4 19), is Claudio's denunciation of Hero. The audience knows that innocent Hero is falsely accused and that Claudio has been deceived, but she is helpless in the face of a battery of accusations (all from men): 'Oh God defend me, how am I beset!/What kind of catechising call you this?' (4.1 71). When she faints, her prone form has considerable dramatic impact – she lies there, the victim of male arrogance and misinterpretation.

Beatrice and Hero

Shakespeare creates Beatrice and Hero as contrasting characters through structure, language and dramatic action. Each one's relationship with a male forms the focus of a different plot: Claudio's near-tragic relationship with Hero forms the main plot whilst Benedick's coming together with Beatrice forms the comic sub-plot. The characters of the two as shown in the opening scenes reflect their respective roles: Hero is conventionally pretty, passive and patient, ready to marry whoever her father wishes, while Beatrice is freer from family ties, fiercely independent in spirit and ready to challenge the attitudes of a male-dominated Messina. Her challenges to Benedick begin even before he appears, and she declares her contempt for men and for marriage to 'a piece of valiant dust.'

Benedick

Benedick, although not part of Shakespeare's sources, belongs to the tradition of those who scorn love but finally surrender to it. Initially he plays the part of the carefree, committed bachelor, self-consciously cynical about women and about love. He boasts of being 'a professed tyrant to their sex' (1.1 124), and the more his friends jest about seeing him 'look pale with love' (1.1 183) the more extravagant becomes his railing against women. Despite (or because of) his past as a womaniser, he is particularly emphatic that he will never marry, and that should he do so he would deservedly be a figure of fun. His protestations are so extreme that audiences realise that Shakespeare is setting him up for future marriage to Beatrice, his apparent antagonist.

In the 'merry war of wit' Benedick often comes off second best to Beatrice. He calls her 'Lady Disdain' and 'My Lady Tongue,' but avoids her at times, not least because he is wounded by her words: she 'speaks poniards' (small, slender daggers) and 'every word stabs' (2.1 187).

Key quotation

One Hero died defiled, but I do live,

And surely as I live, I am a maid.
(Hero, 5.4 64)

Build critical skills

Beatrice gently chides Hero for being too obedient, suggesting that when it comes to choosing a husband she should dare to say, 'Father, as it please me.'

How else does Shakespeare present the differences between Hero and Beatrice in the opening scenes?

Build critical skills

The Prince says that, 'Benedick is not the unhopefullest husband that I know' (2.1 285).
What qualities does Shakespeare give Benedick in the early scenes?

Like Beatrice, Benedick is not given clear social status by Shakespeare – obviously a gentleman (he is called Signor Benedick), he is neither a count like Claudio nor a prince. We hear of 'Signor Benedick' before we see him on stage, but since this is through the eyes of Beatrice we have an image of a man of words rather than of deeds. This is contradicted by the messenger: 'He hath done good service, lady, in these wars' but the early focus is on what Benedick says rather than on what he does. ('I wonder that you will still be talking, Signor Benedick, nobody marks you.')

Benedick is presented as a character who revels in his reputation as a 'professed tyrant' to the opposite sex. He is not a woman-hater, indeed he is proud that (allegedly) he is 'loved of all ladies' except Beatrice, but the more serious Claudio becomes about being in love, the more extreme becomes Benedick's attitude to women: 'Because I will not do them the wrong to mistrust any, I will do myself the right to trust none' (1.1 180–181). He declares that if ever he falls in love, 'hang me in a bottle like a cat, and shoot at me.' As for marriage, should he ever wear the horns of a cuckold (and he implies that all husbands do), 'let them signify under my sign "Here may you see Benedick the married man".' He does of course protest too much, thereby signalling to the audience that marrying him off will be a major part of the play.

It is the language that Shakespeare gives Benedick that creates his character most powerfully in the mind of the audience: witty, sharp at repartee (but not quite as sharp as Beatrice) and capable of conjuring up magnificently exaggerated images such as 'pick out mine eyes with a ballad-maker's pen, and hang me up at the door of a brothel house for the sign of blind Cupid' (1.1 187).

Despite his superficial bravado Benedick is a man of some sensitivity. When Beatrice mocks the disguised Benedick at the masked ball, he is deeply hurt by her insults: 'Oh she misused me past the endurance of a

Key quotations

Benedick:

Here may you see Benedick the married man
(1.1 199)

I do love nothing in the world so well as you, is not that strange?
(4.1 259)

block' (2.1 181). Shakespeare depicts Benedick as older, more intelligent and more emotionally mature than Claudio, so when he challenges Claudio to a duel it has real dramatic impact.

The gulling scene, with Benedick hidden behind the arbour, is one of the comic highlights of the play, but his final coming together with Beatrice in marriage is not merely funny – there is emotional depth in the union of two characters who have been shown to 'deserve' each other. Finally, aware that he usually loses the war of words, he resorts to a kiss to silence Beatrice.

Claudio

Claudio initially fits the stereotype of the courtly lover: a brave young soldier who is rich, noble and ready for love. However his language, with its imagery of the market-place, makes us question the quality of his love for Hero: 'Can the world buy such a jewel?' (1.1 134) and 'Let every eye negotiate for itself,/And trust no agent' (2.1.135). Early on Claudio says 'That I love her, I feel,' but he judges Hero by her looks and asks, 'Is she not a modest young lady?' His other concern does not endear him to an audience – he checks out her inheritance prospects with Don Pedro: 'Hath Leonato any son, my Lord?' (1.1 220).

Claudio's love for Hero has an awkward path from the start – someone else woos her on his behalf. We remember this later when his love turns sour. When Don Pedro hands over Hero, Claudio says little: 'Silence is the perfectest herald of joy'. He is an inexperienced lover, anxious to know what his friends think of Hero, and insecure enough to be instantly suspicious of her when Don John suggests that 'the lady is disloyal'. Even before he is shown some evidence of apparent infidelity Claudio declares, nastily, 'If I see any thing tonight, why I should not marry her tomorrow in the congregation, where I should wed, there will I shame her' (3.3 91).

Shakespeare makes it easy for Claudio to be deceived by Borachio's stratagem, but the audience is aware of his vulnerability since he has already been shown to judge by appearance as he did when falling for Hero. Beatrice's contemptuous name for him, 'Count Comfect' (a mixture of being sweet and being something of nothing), stays in the mind of the audience.

Claudio's conduct in church is bound to alienate any audience, especially since we know of her innocence. Tragedy looms, and his vitriol is vicious: 'you are more intemperate in your blood/Than Venus, or those pampered animals,/That rage in savage sensuality' (4.1 55).

In this scene of near-tragic intensity Shakespeare presents Claudio through what he does, what he says and how others react to him. What he does is intended to maximise Hero's humiliation and what he says

Key quotations

Claudio:

where I should wed,
there will I shame her.
(3.3 91)

Give not this rotten
orange to your friend.
(4.1 27)

Build critical skills

Yet sinned I not but in
mistaking.

(5.1 241)

How does
Shakespeare
present Claudio's
justification for his
conduct towards
Hero?

is savage. He opens with the deadly monosyllable 'No' and when the unsuspecting Leonato 'dares' to answer on his behalf he bursts out bitterly, 'Oh what men dare do! What men may do! What men daily do, not knowing what they do!' Claudio has Hero's apparent infidelity in mind here, but others are uncertain what he means and Claudio prolongs the uncertainty by asking if Leonato will 'Give me this maid your daughter?' before returning her saying, 'Give not this rotten orange to your friend.' He follows this with mocking denunciation of Hero's blushes and then, with considerable dramatic irony, says, 'Oh what authority and show of truth/Can cunning sin cover itself withal!' He is right, but about the wrong people. When bewildered Leonato asks what he means, Claudio at last clarifies his position through negatives: 'Not to be married. Not to knit my soul to an approved wanton.' His denunciation becomes more vicious with 'you are more intemperate in your blood/Than Venus, or those pampered animals, That rage in savage sensuality.' All this to a young woman the audience know to be innocent.

When Benedick challenges Claudio to a duel the difference in moral stature between the two former friends is evident – Claudio is shallow enough to be unaware of the damage he has done and thinks that Benedick cannot be serious. Claudio's move from feeling savage to feeling sorry comes with the same rapidity as his move from love to contempt. What is more difficult for an audience to accept is his feeble self-justification: 'Yet sinned I not but in mistaking.'

Despite his attempts at atonement Claudio never emerges as a worthy husband for Hero, but she does accept him, albeit without words of affection.

Leonato

Shakespeare presents Leonato as caring more about his status than his daughter. Typically for an Elizabethan father he assumes that he has the right to dispose of his daughter in marriage in a way that suits him: he would have been pleased to have her marry Don Pedro but is happy to switch her to Count Claudio. Her personal feelings seem to be of little concern to him since he sees marriage as a social affair. He welcomes the Prince with pompous formality and excessive deference, and is conventional enough to worry that his niece is too outspoken to gain a husband: 'thou wilt never get thee a husband if thou be so shrewd of thy tongue.'

Key quotation

oh she is fallen

Into a pit of ink, that
the wide sea

Hath drops too few to
wash her clean again
(Leonato, 4.1 132–134)

When Hero is denounced in church his concerns are more about himself than about her. He instantly believes the accusations and the word 'I' peppers the passage with self-pity. 'Grieved I, I had but one?' He claims that if she does not die of shame, 'Myself would…strike at thy life' (4.1 119–120).

▲ Hero and Leonato in a 2012 stage production

When seeking to challenge Claudio and the Prince, Leonato is almost a figure of fun, but although fierce verbally he never manages to be more than feeble physically. His forgiveness of Claudio is done generously, but almost with the sense of completing a transaction to secure his own status, free from slander.

Don John

Shakespeare presents Don John as the classic stage villain: a brooding, malevolent presence. Although he is given a degree of motivation — jealousy of Claudio and resentment against his brother the rightful Prince of Arragon — his evil is beyond explanation. He would be pleased to poison everyone: 'Would the cook were a my mind' (1.3 53).

His servant Borachio is more intelligent than his master — it is Borachio who initiates both attempts to cause problems for Claudio and at first Don John does not see the mischievous potential of Borachio's friendship with Margaret.

He does play a part in persuading Claudio and the Prince that Hero is unfaithful, but the real work is done by others. When he realises that the plot has been revealed he is quick to flee, but we learn in the final lines that he has been recaptured.

Dogberry and Verges

Dogberry and Verges (think Laurel and Hardy!) are a major source of comedy, but as well as being dramatically very entertaining, they make a significant contribution to the development of the plot and to the exploration of the theme of deception. The humour is primarily verbal, but also physical: the original part was written for Will Kempe, a famous clown with Shakespeare's company. In many productions there is an entertaining contrast between a bulky, pompous and patronising Dogberry and a doddery, mouse-like Verges: 'A good old man, sir, he will be talking as they say, when the age is in, the wit is out' (3.5 26). No wonder that Leonato finds him 'tedious'.

Dogberry's reach for words exceeds his grasp, so his verbal humour is the opposite of Beatrice and Benedick's accomplished wordplay. Full of self-importance, he tries to use long, significant words but usually and hilariously gets them wrong. He often reverses his intended meaning, as in his briefing of the Watch when he misuses 'allegiance' and confuses 'apprehend' with 'comprehend' or tells the Sexton that he is a 'malefactor'. When he demands to be 'writ down an ass' (4.2 70) the comedy is that he is indeed an ass, but seems not to realise it.

▲ Dogberry and Verges (front row) in an open air production

Dogberry enters just after Don John has spoken of Hero's 'disloyalty' and things have started moving towards a potentially tragic situation. Initially the assembling of the Watch is merely comic, especially for an Elizabethan audience for whom the Watch was a byword for ineffectiveness, but it does not remain just comic. Soon after the audience has heard the beginning of Don John's plot, the plotters are overheard by the Watch, thereby taking some of the tension out of the potentially tragic scenes that follow. Set against that is the tension that grows over whether Dogberry's digressions and verbosity will delay making public the truth for so long that Hero's disgrace might lead to disaster.

Shakespeare used Dogberry to create an image of authority that is laughable and leaves us as audience to apply that thought as widely as we see fit. However, despite the comic incompetence of the Watch, and especially of Dogberry, it is the Watch (not the nobles) who discover the plot to disgrace Hero. Shakespeare did not have that happen by accident: it is another layer of complexity around the idea of deception that it is the foolish yokels who find out the truth whilst their 'betters' are taken in by appearances. At one point, thanks to Dogberry and an uncomprehending constable, the imaginary thief 'Deformed' takes on a life of his own – another example of the unreal being taken to be real.

Key quotations

Dogberry:

you shall comprehend all vagrom men
(3.3 21)

masters, remember that I am an ass.
(4.2 62–63)

REVIEW YOUR LEARNING

(Answers are given on pp. 102–103.)

1   How can you demonstrate in your writing that you remember that characters are constructs, not people?

2   Select three quotations that show different aspects of Claudio's character.

3   Select and comment on two or three dramatic moments which indicate how Benedick's attitude to marriage changes during the play.

4   Choose two quotations that illustrate the differences between Beatrice and Hero.

5   Comment on the ways in which the Watch, Dogberry and Verges contribute to the plot and to the play's humour.

6   How does Shakespeare present Leonato as a father? Comment in detail on two images which reveal different aspects of Leonato's character.

7   Compare and contrast the ways in which the Prince and Don John seek to manipulate other characters.

GRADE *FOCUS*

Grade 5
To achieve Grade 5, students will develop a clear understanding of how and why Shakespeare uses language, form and structure to create characters, supported by appropriate references to the text.

Grade 8
To achieve Grade 8, students will examine and evaluate the ways that Shakespeare uses language form and structure to create characters, supported by carefully chosen and well-integrated references to the text.

Themes

Target your thinking

- What is a theme? (**AO1, AO2, AO3**)
- What are the main themes in *Much Ado About Nothing*? (**AO1, AO3**)
- How are these themes presented and explored by Shakespeare? (**AO2**)
- How might these themes be viewed by different audiences? (**AO3**)

A loose definition of a theme in drama is that it is an idea that the playwright explores throughout a play. If something features only once or twice it would not be sufficiently implanted in the mind of the audience to be called a theme, but the ideas below are returned to again and again in *Much Ado About Nothing*:

1 Appearance and reality

2 Women and men

3 Wisdom and folly

4 Love and marriage

The title *Much Ado About Nothing* had a dual meaning for Shakespeare's original audience: 'nothing' was pronounced as 'no thing' and was therefore very similar to 'noting' or observing. (Don Pedro and Balthasar joke about this in Act 2 scene 3.) This title promised a play of contradictions and double meanings to an Elizabethan audience and it is a play of dualities: people and ideas are not presented in isolation, but in relation to each other – appearance and reality; love and marriage; wisdom and folly and, most obviously, men and women.

Unlike most of Shakespeare's earlier comedies, *Much Ado About Nothing* is a comedy with a deeply serious dimension. The audience is amused in one scene but aghast in the next, and although everything is satisfactorily resolved on the surface, there is a disturbing undercurrent of menace, personified by Don John, which means the ending is not entirely comforting. We leave the theatre with unanswered questions about our loves and our lives.

Appearance and reality

This is the most complex theme because it is about more than the play itself – it is about the nature of the theatre as illusion. The unreal world of the stage is one where ideas and emotions can be presented and explored by actors who are not, in real life, what they appear to be on the stage.

GRADE **BOOSTER**

Turn to pp. 97–98 in the 'Top ten' section for a series of short memorable quotations on the main themes. You will find it useful to have them at your fingertips in the examination.

The image of the world as a theatre appears continually in Shakespeare, most memorably perhaps in Macbeth's image of life as 'a poor player/ That struts and frets his hour upon the stage', or in the speech by Jacques in *As You Like It*:

All the world's a stage,

And all the men and women merely players…

Much Ado About Nothing is set in a Messina full of deceptions, some lighthearted and some malevolent. It is no accident that a pivotal early scene is a masked ball. From an audience perspective it is not as simple as assuming that deception is evil: Don John's deceit may be wicked in intent and initial outcome, but without the deceptions practised on Beatrice and Benedick, would they ever have married?

▲ The masked ball in Branagh's 1993 film adaptation

We quickly learn that things are rarely what they seem in Messina. Claudio seems an honourable young gentleman, smitten by Hero's beauty, but proves otherwise; Beatrice and Benedick appear fiercely hostile to each other and to marriage yet finish as a married couple; Don Pedro woos Hero, not for himself but for Claudio; and Don John may superficially appear reconciled but is driven only by revenge.

Differences between surface and substance are introduced in the opening scene and signal key ideas that will be explored later – the 'young Florentine called Claudio' has 'borne himself beyond the promise of his years' and 'bettered expectation' in terms of bravery since he has done 'in the figure of a lamb the feats of a lion' (1.1 12). His true love and courage will be tested. Beatrice's first reference to Benedick as 'Signor

Mountanto' (suggesting that he is a show-off as a fencer but also given to 'mounting' women), and her promise to eat all those he has killed, may raise questions for the audience about whether his bravery is real or just apparent, and whether her antagonism is assumed or real. One of the lines of development in the play is Beatrice's recognition of Benedick's true worth as a soldier and as a man. Leonato's welcome to Don Pedro is deeply ironic: 'Never came trouble to my house in the likeness of your Grace' (1.1 73) – since Don Pedro's support for Claudio's belief in Hero's illusory betrayal brings great trouble.

Much Ado About Nothing is full of references to seeing and eyesight. Early on Claudio says that Hero is 'the sweetest lady that ever I looked on' (1.1 139) and Don John continues the focus on eyesight: 'If you dare not trust that you see, confess not that you know.'(3.2 88) The plot against Hero is based on seeing and when accusing Hero, Claudio asks, with an irony which the audience would note, 'Are our eyes our own?' His eyes, and those of the Prince, have been deceived by Borachio's manipulation of appearances. It is symbolically significant that penitent Claudio marries the hidden Hero without seeing her – the truth of the heart is shown to be below the surface rather than on the surface. Beatrice and Benedick, by contrast, are deceived by what they hear rather than what they see.

Shakespeare's most entertaining exploration of appearance and reality is in the sub-plot – the light-hearted 'gulling' of Benedick (2.3) into the belief that Beatrice is in love with him, but 'counterfeits' to conceal it. Benedick's response is to admit that 'When I said I would die a bachelor, I did not think I should live till I were married' (2.3 197). Very quickly he is able to 'spy some marks of love in her' (2.3 199) reminding the audience that love is indeed in the eye of the beholder. A parallel deception is practised on Beatrice by Hero and Ursula so that she too is ready to tame her 'wild heart' and to allow Benedick's wooing. Deception here is a source of audience amusement and will give the eventual satisfaction of a marriage of true minds.

By contrast, the deception on which the main plot hinges is hatched in malice and is full of menace. It is the initially successful attempt by Don John and Borachio to deceive Claudio into believing that Hero is unfaithful, and it moves the mood of the play from comedy towards tragedy as Claudio snarls at Leonato 'Give not this rotten orange to your friend' (4.1 27). It is not a coincidence that 'nothing' was also an Elizabethan slang reference to the vagina, and that Claudio's suspicion centres on Hero's loss of virginity.

This potentially tragic situation is rescued, not by wise nobles or brave soldiers as one might expect, but by those figures of fun, the Watch, who may stumble over words but also stumbled over the wickedness behind Don John's deception.

The final deception – the revelation that Claudio's new bride is the reputedly dead Hero – enables the play to end in a positive whirl of weddings. A contemporary or modern audience might reflect, as they leave the world of theatrical illusion, on the different ways appearance and reality in Messina have been manipulated by Shakespeare and how they relate to each other in life.

Women and men

Well, why not 'Women and men' rather than the more frequent 'Men and women'? Possibly because although Elizabethan women were so often defined by their relationship to men, as mother, daughter or wife, yet on the English throne reigned a monarch who was very much her own woman – unmarried Elizabeth I. Not wholly surprising then that in Beatrice Shakespeare has created another of his witty and independent-minded female characters whose audience appeal crosses the centuries, and for contrast, provided the conventionally quiet and submissive Hero. Beatrice has been placed there by Shakespeare because she is different. She is completely Shakespeare's invention: in his sources there was no Beatrice and therefore no contrast. The male/female situation was given an additional dimension by the fact that all the women were played by boys – women were not allowed to perform on the stage in Shakespeare's time.

Beatrice bursts into verbal life in the opening scene, mocking martial valour ('How many has he killed and eaten in these wars?' [1.1 31]) in a way that her uncle Leonato finds somewhat disconcerting since he apologetically explains, 'You must not, sir, mistake my niece'. There is no mistaking that Beatrice's quickness of mind and tongue are a match for any man. She talks so disparagingly of Benedick, as a 'stuffed man' that the messenger observes, 'I see, lady, the gentleman is not in your books,' only to receive the withering response, 'an he were I would burn my study' (1.1 67). The 'merry war of wit' between Beatrice and Benedick is entertainingly evident in their first exchange:

BEATRICE
I wonder that you will still be talking, Signor Benedick, nobody marks you.
BENEDICK
What, my dear Lady Disdain! Are you yet living?

(1.1 86–88)

Their verbal battle launches the sub-plot which eventually brings them together and provides amusement for the audience whilst fulfilling their expectation that the two opponents will eventually marry despite the tensions between male and female. Leonato feels entitled to joke about

Give not this rotten orange to your friend.
(Claudio, 4.1 27)

GRADE BOOSTER

Examination questions may ask you to consider how Shakespeare uses a particular character to present a theme. For example, how does Shakespeare present the theme of appearance and reality through Claudio? Learn to think of characters in this way as one of Shakespeare's techniques for conveying his message.

Build critical skills

Leonato's assumption that he can dispose of his daughter, 'Count, take of me my daughter' (2.1 229) was typical of Shakespeare's time.

What other evidence can you find in the play about the place of women in the society of Messina?

Build critical skills

Beatrice says, 'O God that I were a man! I would eat his heart in the market place.'

How does this image contribute to the theme of men and women?

Build critical skills

I wonder that you will still be talking, Signor Benedick, nobody marks you.

(1.1.86)

Why did Shakespeare present Beatrice as so antagonistic to Benedick in the opening scene?

his wife's fidelity and to give away his daughter, not once, but twice – to Don Pedro, then to Claudio. Don Pedro thinks it appropriate to woo a woman in the name of another man; Borachio assumes (rightly) that he can manipulate Margaret, and Claudio feels justified in humiliating Hero because his manly honour has, he thinks, been besmirched. How can the women retaliate? Only through words or through silent suffering unless a man is prepared to fight their battles for them.

Beatrice's anger with Claudio is a sign of her emotional strength but also of her social and physical weakness, since despite her fury she still needs Benedick as a male champion to tackle Claudio. The situation is further complicated in that Shakespeare made Beatrice's style and language more masculine than was conventional for a young woman. This blurred the gender boundaries even more and forced the audience to think more carefully about socially-determined male/female roles.

The most powerful dramatic moment of the main plot is when Claudio stands hurling abuse at a silent Hero – 'She knows the heat of a luxurious bed:/Her blush is guiltiness not modesty' (4.1 36). It could be argued that Claudio's image of Hero was too idealised ever to match reality, but Hero's reaction is that of a conventional female victim – to plead for a dagger to commit suicide before collapsing in a swoon.

Once Don John's plot is revealed, the emotional authority drains away from the Count and Claudio and rests with Hero's defenders, most notably Beatrice. Claudio and the Count, 'a pair of honourable men' in Leonato's ironic words, are completely humbled: penitent Claudio says, 'Impose me to what penance your invention can lay upon my sin' whilst the duped Don Pedro says he would 'bend under any weight' (5.1 244).

GRADE BOOSTER

When you write about themes, explain and explore how Shakespeare has presented his themes in a range of ways: through the plot, through what is said and through what happens on stage. Give precise examples for each of these in relation to any particular theme. For example, if writing about the theme of women and men, analyse how the pairs of characters are contrasted, how men seem unable to see clearly once honour is involved and how helpless most women (except Beatrice) are in a male-dominated Messina.

Shakespeare offers a challenging exploration of the power relationships between men and women but he reflects the social realities of his time: it is Leonato and Benedick, not Hero and Beatrice, who lead the charge for justice, and the last we see of Beatrice, so voluble in the early scenes and in defence of her cousin, is when her mouth is 'stopped' by Benedick's kiss.

When writing about a theme, remember to point out
that audiences of different times or with different
attitudes might respond differently to the same scene.
Shakespeare's subtle ambiguities enable directors
to emphasise ideas in varying ways whilst still
respecting the text. For example, an all-female cast
in a modern production would give a different take on
the relationships between men and women.

Wisdom and folly

Wisdom and folly in Messina (as perhaps today or in Elizabethan England)
are not linked with straightforward class or gender categories. The men
of high rank behave foolishly in this play, while the high-ranking female
characters do nothing foolish (apart perhaps in Hero's case accepting
Claudio a second time) and sometimes show real insight. The lower-class
buffoons who seem so foolish are the ones to discover the evil plotting of
high-ranking Don John.

The idea of folly was the focus of much writing in the sixteenth century.
The two most obvious examples of folly in the play are different in kind:
Claudio's folly in suspecting and humiliating Hero is folly of near-tragic
intensity which exposes human frailty, whilst Dogberry's self-aggrandising
verbosity is much lighter in tone, combining laugh-aloud humour in his
language with a satirical edge. Claudio's folly is to believe his eyes rather
than his heart. His foolishness is even more apparent to the audience
who see him insulting and degrading Hero when they know that she
is the innocent victim of Don John's evil. His progress towards greater
wisdom and self-knowledge is not entirely convincing – his 'punishment'
is perfunctory and Shakespeare makes him lament rather plaintively that,
'Yet sinned I not but in mistaking.'

Dogberry's verbal follies are a source of delight and he could never be
accused of wisdom, except possibly for his final advice to the Watch to
'watch about Signor Leonato's door'. Shakespeare's ironic touch is to
make the discovery of the plot depend on Dogberry's 'foolish' Watch
rather than on the supposed wisdom of the nobles.

Both Beatrice and Benedick claim that it is wisdom to stay single and
folly to marry. Benedick puts forward his case against marriage in pseudo-
logical fashion: 'Because I will not do them the wrong to mistrust any, I
will do myself the right to trust none' (1.1 180). Similarly, Beatrice argues,
with apparent logic, that 'Adam's sons are my brethren and, truly, I hold it
a sin to match with my kindred' (2.1 46). When they eventually surrender
to marriage such folly seems like wisdom to the audience.

Build critical skills

These words of
Dogberry's during
the examination
of Conrade and
Borachio are a
mix of truth and
nonsense: 'Why this
is flat perjury to call
a prince's brother
villain.'

Can you find other
examples where
Dogberry's words
are not entirely
foolish?

Key quotation

*What your wisdoms
could not discover,
these shallow fools
have brought to light.*
(Borachio, 5.1 205)

49

Love and marriage

Much Ado About Nothing is an exploration of love through actions and through words. The play has marriage as its destination, as required by the tradition of such romantic comedies, but the use of contrasting pairs of lovers makes the journey to that destination an intriguing one. Shakespeare sets the play after a war when peace makes possible a focus on feelings rather than fighting. Claudio claims that 'war thoughts have left their places vacant' and that instead 'come thronging soft and delicate desires' (1.1 228). He says of Hero that initially he 'looked upon her with a soldier's eye' (1.1 224) but that he 'liked her ere I went to wars.'(1.1 231)

By bringing the idea of a 'war of words' into the opening scene Shakespeare extends the imagery of war into what is shown as a battle between the sexes. The main combatants are Beatrice, who 'speaks poniards, and every word stabs' (2.1 187) and Benedick who has been a 'professed tyrant' to women. Military imagery is also there in Don Pedro's claiming that when wooing Hero he will 'take her hearing prisoner with the force/And strong encounter of my amorous tale' (1.1 250–251). Shakespeare's audience would not have found it strange that Don Pedro woos Hero on behalf of Claudio, but modern audiences may see it as a doubtful start to a relationship.

Shakespeare's presentation of the theme of romantic love is full of irony: the passionate young lover Claudio swings rapidly to hating Hero and their marriage is symbolic rather than emotionally significant. Meanwhile the two mature lovers, Beatrice and Benedick, are brought together only by the lies of others. Their love for each other is immediate and amusing – Benedick is determined to be 'horribly in love with her' (2.3 191) while Beatrice, on hearing that she is beloved is instantly ready to 'bind our loves up in a holy band' (3.1 114).

Claudio's youthful love for Hero is based almost entirely on visual appeal – 'In mine eye she is the sweetest lady that ever I looked on' (1.1 139) – so it is appropriate that it is Claudio's eyes that deceive him into believing that Hero is unfaithful. By contrast, Beatrice claims 'I have a good eye, Uncle, I can see a church by daylight' (2.1 59) and with Beatrice and Benedick, their eventual union is a true meeting of minds which is much more than skin deep. Dramatically Shakespeare makes sure that the audience's feelings remain focused on Beatrice and Benedick. He does this in part by making Beatrice such a complex character and such a witty critic of conventional assumptions about love and marriage which she describes as 'wooing, wedding and repenting'. Her image of courtship is of an elaborate sequence of dances: 'a scotch jig, a measure and a cinquepace' (2.1 29). In some ways dancing is an appropriate image for

Build critical skills

A miracle! Here's our own hands against our hearts. Come, I will have thee, but by this light I take thee for pity.

(Benedick, 5.4 92)

These words are from the final scene. How has Benedick shown earlier that his love for Beatrice is more than pity?

the play as a whole since it features partners moving towards each other, then away, then coming together at the end.

▲ Beatrice and Benedick in Branagh's 1993 film adaptation

Marriage is the conventional conclusion for a romantic text. (Think of Charlotte Bronte's final chapter of Jane Eyre which begins, 'Reader, I married him.') However in *Much Ado About Nothing* the final marriages are not idealised and it is hard to think that the characters will live happily married ever after. The image of marriage that Shakespeare presents in the final scene is, in Benedick's term, 'enigmatical'. During the play marriage has been seen by Claudio, Leonato and Don Pedro as a goal to be desired, but by Beatrice and by Benedick who 'railed so long against marriage' (2.3 194) as a suffering to be avoided. The audience, who have expected marriage to be the inevitable culmination of a romantic comedy, feel, like Antonio, 'glad that all things sort so well' (5.4 7) but Benedick's request to the Friar is 'to bind me or undo me' (5.4 20) suggesting that marriage is a constraint, yet he refers to 'the state of honourable marriage'. Claudio is ready to marry anyone as his penance – again not a ringing endorsement of marriage as the result of true love – and his next joking reference to 'lusty Jove' suggests images of rape rather than marital union based on mutual affection. Hero's acceptance of him is a declaration of her innocence rather than her love: 'I am a maid.' The union of Beatrice and Benedick, who take each other laughingly on sufferance, offers a more positive pairing since they make no inflated claims and love each other 'no more than reason' (5.4 78).

At the end Hero accepts Claudio, as she must, but utters no words of love. However since neither Beatrice nor Benedick has illusions about the

Build critical skills

What image of marriage does Shakespeare present in the final scene?

since I do purpose to marry, I will think nothing to any purpose that the world can say against it.

(Benedick, 5.4 101)

other, there is hope for their marriage. When she first hears that Benedick loves her Beatrice says she will try, 'taming my wild heart to thy loving hand' and talks immediately in terms of marriage: 'If thou dost love, my kindness shall incite thee/To bind our loves up in a holy band' (3.1 111). At the end Beatrice agrees only to 'yield upon great persuasion, and partly to save your life, for I was told you were in a consumption' (5.4 94). Benedick's passion is similarly managed with a dash of mockery: 'by this light I take thee for pity' (5.4.92). Benedick dares to advise the Prince, 'Get thee a wife, get thee a wife' but adds jokingly that any wife will be unfaithful and give her husband the horns of a cuckold, and therefore that 'there is no staff more reverend than one tipped with horn' (5.4 115).

Shakespeare's exploration of love and marriage is characteristically complex. He presents conventional views for and against marriage, yet undercuts both. The fiercest critics of marriage seem more likely to succeed as a married couple than the young lovers whose affection is grounded only in physical attraction.

GRADE *FOCUS*

Grade 5

To achieve Grade 5, students will reveal a clear understanding of the key themes of the play and how Shakespeare uses language, form and structure to explore them, supported by appropriate references to the text.

Grade 8

To achieve Grade 8, students will be able to examine and evaluate the key themes of the play, analyzing the ways that Shakespeare uses language, form and structure to explore them. Comments will be supported by carefully chosen and well-integrated references to the text.

GRADE *BOOSTER*

Most questions are not on themes themselves but on how Shakespeare 'presents' those themes. For example, the task might be to analyse how the playwright presents a theme in a particular extract and then in the play as a whole. Because the task is focused on Shakespeare's methods, not just on a theme, it would be relevant to include analysis of language, structure, character and context.

REVIEW YOUR LEARNING

(Answers are given on p. 103.)

1 What is a theme?

2 What are the main themes of *Much Ado About Nothing?*

3 Find three quotations that contribute to Shakespeare's exploration of the theme of appearance and reality.

4 How does Shakespeare present the women's different reactions in the scene where Claudio denounces Hero?

5 Choose three dramatic moments that show different types of folly in *Much Ado About Nothing.*

6 Find two or three quotations which show how Benedick's attitude to marriage changes during the play.

Language, style and analysis

Target your thinking

- When does Shakespeare use prose rather than verse? (**AO2**)
- What is the impact of imagery in the play? (**AO2**)
- What literary techniques does Shakespeare use? (**AO2**)
- How do wit and humour contribute to the play? (**AO2**)

You will notice from the questions above that when analysing language and style, the Assessment Objective with which we are most concerned is AO2, which refers to the writer's methods and is usually highlighted in the exam question by the word 'how'. Language and style are of vital importance since they are the means by which writers help to create our understanding of plot, character and themes.

Examiners report that AO2 is the Assessment Objective most often overlooked by students in the examination. For example, candidates who fail to address AO2 often write about the characters in a play as if they were real people involved in real events rather than analysing them as 'constructs' or creations of the writer.

Prose and verse

Only one of Shakespeare's plays, *The Merry Wives of Windsor*, has a higher percentage of prose to verse than *Much Ado About Nothing*. Verse was traditionally used for noble characters and great events so it is appropriate that Shakespeare chose to use prose for over two-thirds of this entertainingly earthy play.

Generally it is a combination of the character and the nature of the scene that determines Shakespeare's choice of verse or prose. Some characters, particularly the high-status ones like Leonato, Don Pedro and Claudio, speak verse as well as prose, switching as the tenor of the scene changes. When things are casual and amusing they tend to use prose, but the more serious a dramatic situation the more likely it is that they will speak in verse. For example, in Act 2 scene 1 Claudio, pretending to be Benedick, speaks prose in his exchange with Don John, switches to verse to express his anguish that the Prince is wooing Hero and returns to prose for his conversation with jesting Benedick. Some characters, especially the low-life Watch, but also Don John despite his noble(ish) birth, always speak prose.

Nothing is what it first seems in Messina, even the language, which seems so spontaneous yet is so carefully constructed. Shakespeare has the romantic lovers, Claudio and Hero, speaking in blank verse – unrhymed verse with ten beats per line (iambic pentameters). This is to contrast their lofty, idealised sentiments with the earthier prose of Beatrice or Benedick. For example, in the first scene Claudio talks with Don Pedro of 'thronging soft and delicate desires,/All prompting me how fair young Hero is' (1.1 227); these rhetorical flourishes sound more artificial since only minutes earlier Benedick had been saying, 'she's too low for a high praise, too brown for a fair praise, and too little for a great praise' (1.1 126).

Shakespeare has Beatrice speaking prose early on in the play, and when she is bandying insults with Benedick there is often a scornful tone to the words: 'I had rather hear my dog bark at a crow than a man swear he loves me' (1.1 97). The first time that she speaks in verse is when she learns of Benedick's love for her. Her mood is no longer one of witty verbal jousting as she speaks in rhyming verse:

> What fire is in mine ears? Can this be true?
> Stand I condemned for pride and scorn so much?
> Contempt, farewell, and maiden pride, adieu,
> No glory lies behind the back of such.
>
> (3.1 107)

The masked ball scene provides a useful example of Shakespeare's switching between verse and prose. It begins with characters exchanging repartee in prose. Claudio is masked but is recognised by Don John who pretends that he thinks Claudio is Benedick in order to plant the unwelcome news that Don Pedro is wooing Hero for himself. The switching sequence is then as follows:

1 Claudio responds in prose during their conversation: 'How know you he loves her?'

2 However, as soon as he is alone Shakespeare has him switch to blank verse:

> Friendship is constant in all other things
> Save in the office and affairs of love;
> Therefore all hearts in love use their own tongues.

This enables him to express the heightened emotion of his initial distress.

3 When he is joined by Benedick in a typical mood of male banter Claudio says little, but says in prose: 'I pray you, leave me.'

When Claudio accuses Hero, Shakespeare has him do so in blank verse, befitting for the seriousness and emotional intensity of the scene.

> You seem to me as Dian in her orb,
> As chaste as is the bud ere it be blown;
> But you are more intemperate in your blood
> Than Venus, or those pampered animals,
> That rage in savage sensuality.
>
> (4.1 53)

Build critical skills

Why does Shakespeare have Claudio switch between prose and verse in Act 2 scene 1?

Others too speak in verse here, making this an untypical scene in terms of language style. Only when the others have left Beatrice and Benedick alone together and the mood of the scene lightens a little is prose used.

Relationships and tensions between men and women are at the heart of the play, and this is signalled by the choice of prose or verse for the gulling scenes. Males and females make very different verbal music since Benedick is deceived in prose whilst Hero and Ursula speak blank verse whilst entrapping Beatrice.

Imagery

Imagery is not confined to verse: the prose of the play is full of images used to create deliberate effects in the imagination of the audience and illuminate key themes of the play. For example, in the opening scene Claudio refers to Hero as a 'jewel', a precious object with a market value, which can be bought and sold. The images they use reveal that the male characters think of women as possessions to be owned rather than people to be loved. We realise that what matters most to Claudio is outward appearance when he says, in the language of the market, 'Let every eye negotiate for itself'.

Food references are frequent. Before we see him, we hear that Benedick, according to Beatrice, is 'a very valiant trencherman', given to fighting food rather than foes. Claudio's words are deemed by Benedick to be 'a fantastical banquet, just so many strange dishes' whilst Benedick himself thinks 'love may transform me to an oyster' (2.3 17–19). He also thinks that the appetite can alter: 'A man loves the meat in his youth that he cannot endure in his age.'

As pointed out in the 'Context' section (p. 14) *Much Ado About Nothing* is full of everyday images of birds and animals from the Elizabethan countryside. For example, Claudio is 'a poor hurt fowl' whilst Beatrice 'like a lapwing, runs' (3.1 24). In the exchange below Benedick and Beatrice trade verbal blows in terms of animals with images of a chattering parrot, a cantering horse and finally a misbehaving horse (jade):

BENEDICK

Well, you are a rare parrot-teacher.

BEATRICE

A bird of my tongue is better than a beast of yours.

BENEDICK

I would my horse had the speed of your tongue, and so good a continuer.

BEATRICE

You always end with a jade's trick.

In the gulling scene
Claudio whispers
in an aside that
Benedick has 'ta'en
th'infection.'

What dramatic
impact does this
image of disease
have on an
audience?

Reflecting the Elizabethan excitement about exploration, Shakespeare has Benedick draw his images from around the world. Rather than meet Beatrice he would 'fetch you a tooth-picker now from the furthest inch of Asia' or 'fetch you a hair off the Great Cham's beard'. By contrast Shakespeare has Beatrice using much more local images at times – we admire her imagination when she twists the biblical idea that man is but dust into a comic image that punctures male pretensions:

> Would it not grieve a woman to be overmastered with a piece of valiant dust? to make an account of her life to a clod of wayward marl?
>
> (2.1 43–45)

Fashion was likely to be something very much in the minds of the original audience. It is a particularly rich source of images in the play, not least because it links with the theme of outward appearance versus inner truth. Beatrice is scathing in advance about Benedick – 'he wears his faith but as the fashion of his hat, it ever changes with the next block' (1.1 55) – and he is described by Don Pedro as a follower of contemporary fashion who changes styles so rapidly because he has 'a fancy to this foolery' (3.2 28). Fashion features most strongly as an image at a key moment of the play: it sounds like a person (personification) rather than just an image when Borachio says, 'what a deformed thief this fashion is.'

Literary techniques

One key to
gaining high
marks when
writing about
Shakespeare's
language
choices lies in
explaining what
language does
dramatically.
Analyse and
explore how
particular
words, or their
recurrence,
contribute to
the audience's
perception of
a character or
theme.

When you write about literary techniques remember that what examiners are looking for is an understanding of the effect that those techniques would have had in the theatre. Your mindset needs to be focused on impact, rather than identification: that means not just saying that something is a metaphor, but explaining what the impact of the comparison behind the metaphor might be on the audience.

Many of Shakespeare's literary techniques, employed throughout the play, are visible in Benedick's expostulation (2.1 181–197) after he has been insulted by Beatrice while dancing in disguise, as demonstrated in the table below:

> Oh she misused me past the endurance of a block: an oak but with one green leaf on it, would have answered her: my very visor began to assume life, and scold with her: she told me, not thinking I had been myself, that I was the prince's jester, that I was duller than a great thaw; huddling jest upon jest, with such impossible conveyance upon me that I stood like a man at a mark, with a whole army shooting at me: she speaks poniards, and every word stabs: if her breath were as terrible as her terminations, there were no living near her, she would infect to the north star: I would not marry her,

though she were endowed with all that Adam had left him before he transgressed: she would have made Hercules have turned spit, yea, and have cleft his club to make the fire too: come, talk not of her: you shall find her the infernal Ate in good apparel. I would to God some scholar would conjure her; for certainly, while she is here, a man may live as quiet in hell, as in a sanctuary, and people sin upon purpose, because they would go thither; so indeed all disquiet, horror and perturbation follows her.

Technique	Example	Effect
Simile (a comparison using the words 'as' or 'like') (**Explicitly** linking two different images)	'like a man at a mark, with a whole army shooting at me.'	We imagine Benedick's war of words as a real battle, against overwhelming odds. This reinforces the image of him as a brave soldier facing overwhelming odds and deserving our sympathy. Military imagery is unsurprisingly evident early on, given that the play starts with the ending of a war, but it is also part of the battle of the sexes and the 'skirmish of wit' between Beatrice and Benedick.
Metaphor (a comparison which says something is something else) (**Implicitly** linking two different images)	'she speaks poniards and every word stabs'	We see Beatrice's words as weapons, pricking Benedick painfully with each word. Again we are invited to sympathise with him as a result.
Personification (giving human attributes to non-human objects or ideas)	'my very visor began to assume life'	We imagine Benedick's mask becoming so indignant that it argues with Beatrice. She sounds unreasonable beyond endurance, thus forfeiting the audience's sympathy.
Alliteration (use of the same letter or sound at the start of words that occur close together)	'If her breath were as terrible as her terminations'	The repeated 't' sound is sharp and forceful as Benedick almost spits it out to express his feelings. Later Benedick will be described as having 'a February face so full of frost' (5.4 41)
Exaggeration	'There were no living near her, she would infect the north star'	One of Benedick's verbal habits is exaggeration, humorous on Shakespeare's part of course, but also on Benedick's. Benedick claims that had Beatrice's breaths matched her thoughts, and had they been diseases, they would have spread infection as far as the stars.
Listing	'all disquiet, horror and perturbation follows her.'	This cumulative list piles noun upon noun to convey the trouble that Beatrice (allegedly) causes. Shakespeare increases the number of syllables to intensify the horror, finishing with the four syllables of perturbation. →

Technique	Example	Effect
Biblical references	'Adam, sanctuary, heaven and hell'	References to the Bible and religion link Beatrice with the fall of man in the garden of Eden, and (absurdly but amusingly) build the masked ball into an arena of spiritual conflict.
Classical allusions	Hercules and Ate	The allusions, which endow Beatrice with terrifying legendary power, link the characters with the great figures of classical mythology. This is a disproportion the audience would find intellectually entertaining.

Extended comparison

In addition to using similes and metaphors, Shakespeare sometimes presents an elaborate comparison which is explored in humorous detail, as by Beatrice in Act 2 scene 1 lines 52–57:

> For, hear me, Hero: wooing, wedding, and repenting, is as a Scotch jig, a measure, and a cinquepace: the first suit is hot and hasty, like a Scotch jig (and full as fantastical), the wedding, mannerly modest (as a measure) full of state and ancientry; and then comes Repentance, and with his bad legs falls into the cinquepace faster and faster, till he sink into his grave.

The audience is expected to appreciate the intellectual skill (wit) shown in the scale and detail of the comparison of married life to a sequence of dances. The first phase (wooing) is exciting and 'fantastical' like a fast jig; the second (wedding) is measured and follows the rules whilst the third (repenting) is a dance to death.

Antithesis

Much Ado About Nothing is a play of dualities. Not surprising then that one of the significant linguistic features is antithesis – the balancing of one thing against another, as in this speech by Benedick where the antithesis gives the impression of a balanced judgement, although it is nothing of the kind:

> That I neither feel how she should be loved, nor know how she should be worthy, is the opinion that fire cannot melt out of me
>
> (1.1 171–172)

Leonato's later speech, again using antithesis, is a more menacing judgement with lives at stake:

> I know not: if they speak but truth of her,
> These hands shall tear her, if they wrong her honour,
> The proudest of them shall well hear of it.
>
> (4.1 183–185)

Dramatic irony

Irony used for dramatic effect is when characters are shown as unaware of the impact of their words. For example, a comic use of dramatic irony is in Benedick's protestations against the possibility of his ever being married when the audience know that he is bound to marry in the end.

> let them signify under my sign 'Here you may see Benedick the married man.'

A much more serious example of dramatic irony is Claudio's outburst in the church when the audience, unlike Claudio, know that 'seeming' is responsible for his suspicion of Hero:

> Out on thee! Seeming! I will write against it!

Wit and humour

Much of the humour in the play lies in its language. To be witty as a playwright in Elizabethan times was to use language cleverly and, as in the case of *Much Ado About Nothing*, to pay the audience the compliment of believing that they would get the joke.

The 'skirmish of wit' between Beatrice and Benedick consists of apparently spontaneous wordplay, full of puns and double meanings which have been cleverly crafted by Shakespeare. One example of Shakespeare's linguistic creativity is Beatrice's remark, 'God help the noble Claudio, if he hath caught the Benedick. It will cost him a thousand pound ere a be cured.' Benedick's name echoes the name of the Benedictines, a monastic order, yet it sounds as if it has become a sexually transmitted disease that will cost a fortune to cure.

Often the wordplay is not just amusing — it illuminates the themes of the play. One of the most significant puns in the play is Beatrice's joke on 'civil' and 'Seville': as Shakespeare's audience would know, Seville oranges are bitter and at that time orange/yellow was associated with jealousy.

> The count is neither sad, nor sick, nor merry, nor well; but civil, count, civil as an orange, and something of that jealous complexion.
>
> (2.1 223)

The image of an orange returns, bitter indeed, in Claudio's cruel words to Leonato: 'Give not this rotten orange to your friend.' Hero is reduced to a piece of rotten fruit.

Most Shakespearean puns depend on the same word having different meanings (as in 'noting'). For example, when Shakespeare has Beatrice ask after 'Signor Mountanto' he is expecting the audience to pick up the double meaning — 'mountanto' is a term for an upward thrust in fencing, but its bawdy meaning is an upward thrust of a very different kind. Similarly when the messenger says that Benedick is 'stuffed with all honourable virtues' and Beatrice replies that 'he is no less than a stuffed man'. The messenger's meaning is that Benedick is full of virtues, whilst Shakespeare has Beatrice use the word's other meaning — stuffed like a scarecrow or tailor's dummy — and therefore not capable of fighting.

In the exchange below from the end of the gulling scene, the two meanings of 'pains' (making an effort and feeling pain) are the basis of an unremarkable pun, but the dramatic effect is to make the audience think about the pains and pangs of the love that is already shown as growing between these two characters.

BENEDICK

Fair Beatrice, I thank you for your pains.

BEATRICE

I took no more pains for those thanks than you take pains to thank me: if it had been painful, I would not have come.

(2.3 202–204)

Running jokes

A running joke (or gag) is an amusing joke or a comical reference that appears repeatedly throughout a play. A frequent running joke in Shakespeare, and especially in *Much Ado About Nothing,* is of a *cuckold*: a man whose wife is unfaithful. The word refers to a cuckoo, a bird that lays its eggs in other birds' nests. The cuckold was said to grow horns on his head, invisible to him, but obvious to everyone else. Words and symbols which would suggest cuckolding to Shakespeare's audience include horns, rams, and bulls. In *Much Ado,* the preoccupation with cuckolding begins early in Act 1 scene 1:

DON PEDRO

I think this is your daughter?

LEONATO

Her mother hath many times told me so.

BENEDICK

Were you in doubt, sir, that you asked her?

LEONATO

Signor Benedick, no, for then were you a child.

This scene includes three more references by Benedick to cuckolding, since Shakespeare was emphasising that Benedick's attitude to marriage is that to be married is to be a cuckold — a view shaped by his past as a bachelor and his fear of being cuckolded by men like himself, but also one that will add to the merriment when (inevitably) Shakespeare has him choose to marry. When that happens Benedick returns to the cuckold theme: 'Get thee a wife. There is no staff more reverend than one tipped with horn.'

Whilst Beatrice, Benedick and the other nobles distort language intentionally, Dogberry wrestles continually with words and meanings, and is usually thrown without realising it, much to the amusement of the audience. His talent for using the wrong word (malapropism) is immediately apparent as he chooses 'the most desertless man' for the Watch – he means 'deserving' – and bids the constable 'comprehend all vagrom men' when he means 'apprehend all vagrants.'

Having asserted his right to be called an ass, his triumphant final exit is accompanied by the words, 'I humbly give you leave to depart; and if a merry meeting may be wished, God prohibit it!' Shakespeare's original audience would have loved lines like these, especially when spoken by Will Kempe, the famous clown of Shakespeare's company of players.

GRADE *BOOSTER*

Make a collection of your favourite comic quotations with brief notes. Research has shown that many students find it easier to remember something that makes them laugh. You may also wish to check the 'Top ten' section on p. 95 where you will find lists of quotations on characters, themes and Shakespeare's techniques.

Dogberry is not the only Shakespearean low-life character to stumble hilariously over his words: Juliet's Nurse in *Romeo and Juliet* and Bottom in *A Midsummer Night's Dream* also use what later came to be called malapropisms – ludicrous misuses of words. What gives Dogberry's mistakes their comic edge is the pompous pride he has in his verbal vacuities. He appears foolish by striving to seem sophisticated in his choice of vocabulary. Shakespeare's original audience would have appreciated the humour, but might also have realised that Dogberry's word-mangling was not 'altogether fool' as when he asks, at the start of the examination of the two villains, 'Is our whole dissembly appeared?' He means 'assembly, yet 'dissembling' (pretending or falsifying) is exactly what Borachio has done. The accidental revelation of truth – which happens in the plot of the play – happens here through the language.

Some of the bawdy references in the play, and there are many, are clear enough to a modern audience – 'hang me up at the door of a brothel-house for the sign of blind Cupid' – but some in a modern audience might struggle with remarks that were witty when they were written, such as the cuckold reference 'pluck off the bull's horns and set them in my forehead'. Such bawdiness continually reminds us that this is a play about the physicality of the relationships between men and women. For example, Beatrice deliberately misinterprets Don Pedro's comment about Benedick that she has 'put him down' and quips that 'So I would not he should do me, my lord, lest I should prove the mother of fools'.

Build critical skills

What is the likely impact on an audience of Dogberry's questions here?

Dost thou not suspect my place? Dost thou not suspect my years?

Build critical skills

Why do you think Shakespeare created a character like Dogberry who mixes up his words so much? Think particularly of how he describes himself: 'But, masters, remember that I am an ass.'

Key quotations

I cannot endure my Lady Tongue.
(Benedick, 2.1 186)

Oh that he were here to write me down an ass!
(Dogberry, 4.2 61)

61

GRADE BOOSTER

Remember that examiners expect you to do more than just name linguistic techniques: what matters for higher levels is explaining and exploring the effect those techniques might have on an audience. Focus your answer on specific words and how the way they have been used contributes to the dramatic impact of a particular moment.

GRADE FOCUS

Grade 5

Examiners will expect work at this grade to focus on the question asked and make some relevant points, however general (e.g. Benedick is indignant with Beatrice), when writing about how Shakespeare uses language to present character. You should write about specific words and their effects, and include quotations from the text to prove each point.

Grade 8

To aim for this higher grade, responses need to demonstrate an appreciation of the nuances of Shakespeare's language and the particular impact they have on an audience. You also need to explore and analyse how language contributes to the presentation of characters and ideas. Your argument needs to be based on the analysis of detailed textual evidence and to explore the impact of the language Shakespeare chose to use.

REVIEW YOUR LEARNING

(Answers are given on p. 103.)

1 Find two or three examples which show how the use of prose and/or verse contributes to the play's impact on an audience.

2 Select a simile and a metaphor that show how is imagery used to explore some of the play's key themes.

3 How does Dogberry's language contribute to the comic enjoyment of the play?

4 What is meant by *antithesis*? Find an example.

5 What is 'witty' about the play's dialogue in the opening scene?

6 Why is fashion an important image?

7 How does the way they speak influence the presentation of two different characters?

8 Find two or three examples of how differences between the language of men and of women in the play might influence an audience.

Your response to a question on *Much Ado About Nothing* will be assessed in a 'closed book' English Literature examination. This means that you are not allowed to take a copy of the text into the examination room. Different examination boards arrange their testing of *Much Ado About Nothing* in different ways, so it is vital that you know which paper includes Shakespeare, to enable you to be well prepared on the day of the examination.

Marking

The marking of your responses varies according to the board your school or you have chosen. Each exam board will have a slightly different mark scheme, consisting of a ladder of levels. The marks you achieve in each part of the examination will be converted to your final overall grade. Grades are numbered from 1 to 9, with 9 being the highest. It is important that you familiarise yourself with the relevant mark scheme(s) for your examination. After all, how can you do well unless you know exactly what is required? Assessment Objectives for individual assessments are explained in the next section of the guide (see p. 74).

It is a sign of its significance that with most exam boards the Shakespeare play is the first question on the first English Literature paper. Knowing that you are well prepared for that question is a good way to launch into the exam as a whole. The suggestions below are relevant for all the exam boards because they have much in common in terms of assessment.

Approaching the examination question

How the exam boards assess Shakespeare

Remember that whichever exam board you are taking the question will have been designed to assess the objectives set out in the specification. Question styles differ across the boards, as does the arrangement of the Assessment Objectives (AOs). (See 'Assessment Objectives and skills', p. 74.)

Most of the boards will require you to respond to and analyse a particular passage as well as writing about the play as a whole. Only OCR offers that as an option rather than a requirement. Since you will not know in advance which passage will be chosen, you need to be ready to write about any passage in the play.

The table below gives you information about how Shakespeare is assessed by the different boards.

	AQA	Edexcel	WJEC/Eduqas	OCR
Paper and section	Paper 1 Section A	Paper 1 Section A	Component (Paper) 1 Section A	Paper 2 Section B
Question type	Extract-based question requiring response to an aspect of the extract and response to the same or similar aspect in the play as a whole.	Two-part question. Part (a) is based on an extract. Part (b) asks for a response to an aspect elsewhere in the play.	Two-part question. Part (a) is based on an extract. Part (b) asks for a response to some aspect of the play as a whole.	A choice of two questions on each play. One question refers to an extract. The second question is about an aspect of the play as a whole.
Closed book?	Yes	Yes	Yes	Yes
Choice of question?	No	No	No	Yes
Paper and section length	Paper 1: 1 hour 45 minutes. Section A around 50–55 minutes.	Paper 1: 1 hour 45 minutes. Section A around 50–55 minutes.	Paper 1: 2 hours. Section A around 1 hour.	Paper 2: 2 hours. Section B around 45–50 minutes.
% of grade	34 marks out of 64 for paper. 22% of Literature grade.	40 marks out of 80 for paper. 25% of Literature grade.	40 marks out of 80 for paper. 20% of Literature grade.	40 marks out of 80 for paper. 25% of Literature grade.
AOs assessed	AO1, AO2, AO3, AO4	AO1, AO2, AO3	AO1, AO2, AO4 (not AO3)	AO1, AO2, AO3, AO4
Is AO4 assessed?	Yes. 4 marks out of 34 for Section A.	No	Yes, via part (b) of Section A questions.	Yes. 4 marks out of 40 for Section B.

Types of questions

Styles of questioning vary across the boards as you will see from the examples on pages 65–66. Make sure that you know what to expect from the board you are sitting.

AQA question format

Read the following extract from Act 5 scene 1 of *Much Ado About Nothing* and then answer the question that follows.

At this point in the play Leonato is beginning to think that Hero has been betrayed.

Starting with this conversation, explain how you think Shakespeare presents Leonato as a father.

Write about:

- how Shakespeare presents Leonato in this extract
- how Shakespeare presents Leonato as a father in the play as a whole.

[30 + 4 marks]

WJEC/Eduqas question format

Answer both part (a) and part (b).
You are advised to spend about 20 minutes on part (a), and about 40 minutes on part (b).

(a) Read the extract on the opposite page.

How does Shakespeare create tension for an audience here? Refer closely to details from the extract to support your answer.

[15 marks]

*(b) How does Shakespeare present relationships between men and women in *Much Ado About Nothing*?

[25 marks]

*5 of this question's marks are allocated for accuracy in spelling, punctuation and the use of vocabulary and sentence structures.

Part (a) of this question assesses only AO1 and AO2.

Part (b) of this question assesses AO1, AO2 and AO4 (5 additional marks).

OCR question format

EITHER

10 Explore how Claudio behaves towards Hero. Refer to this extract from Act 4 scene 1 and elsewhere in the play.

OR

11 To what extent does Shakespeare present Beatrice and Hero as contrasting characters? Explore at least two moments from the play to support your ideas.

[40 marks]

Edexcel question format

Much Ado About Nothing – from Act 4 scene 1, lines 25 to 56

In this extract, after Claudio accuses Hero of being unfaithful, Beatrice asks Benedick to kill Claudio.

(a) Explore how Shakespeare presents the idea of dishonour in this extract.

Refer closely to the extract in your answer.

[20 marks]

(b) In this extract, we see a confrontation between the characters.

Explain the importance of confrontations elsewhere in the play.

In your answer you must consider:

- how confrontation is shown
- the consequences of one or two key confrontations

You should refer to the context of the play in your answer.

[20 marks]

Spot the differences!

- Only OCR offers a choice of questions.
- Only AQA uses the phrase 'the play as a whole' and marks the two-part question as a whole.
- Edexcel and WJEC/Eduqas have a different focus for part (a) and for part (b).
- Only OCR has the Shakespeare question in Section B.
- All the boards except Edexcel assess AO4 via Shakespeare.
- Only WJEC/Eduqas allocates more marks to part (b) than to part (a).
- Only WJEC/Eduqas does not assess AO3 (Context) via Shakespeare.

Timing matters

Once the exam starts you will have about 50 minutes in which to plan and write your answer. The first five to ten minutes are the most important. In that time you analyse the question carefully, work out what it is asking you to do and create your plan. In the final few minutes you check that your conclusion relates back to the key point of the question. (Never try to twist the question to the one that you have spent hours revising or the one that you did brilliantly on in your mock exam.)

How to read the question

It seems obvious that you need to read the question carefully to make sure you understand what the task requires, but it is not an easy thing to do: reading the question is a complex process.

The example below is typical of AQA's style of Shakespeare question but the process of reading applies across the boards. That process has been 'unpacked' for you.

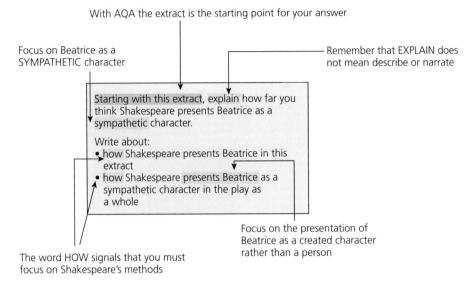

With AQA the extract is the starting point for your answer

Focus on Beatrice as a SYMPATHETIC character

Remember that EXPLAIN does not mean describe or narrate

Starting with this extract, explain how far you think Shakespeare presents Beatrice as a sympathetic character.

Write about:
• how Shakespeare presents Beatrice in this extract
• how Shakespeare presents Beatrice as a sympathetic character in the play as a whole

Focus on the presentation of Beatrice as a created character rather than a person

The word HOW signals that you must focus on Shakespeare's methods

In the exam, as in the example above, it is useful to underline or highlight the key words. They should form the basis of your answer.

Once you have understood the question, read the extract again, underlining or highlighting any words or short phrases that you think might be related to the focus of the question and are of special interest. For example, they might be surprising, unusual or amusing. You might have a strong emotional or analytical reaction to them or you might think that they are particularly clever or noteworthy. These words/phrases may work together to produce a particular effect, to get you to think about a particular theme or to explore the methods the writer uses to present a character in a particular way for their own purposes. You may pick out examples of literary techniques such as lists, the use of imagery, or sound effects such as alliteration or onomatopoeia.

You may spot an unusual word order or sentence construction. The important thing to remember is that when you start writing you must try to *explain* the effects created by these words/phrases or techniques, and not simply identify what they mean. Above all, ensure that you are answering the question.

How to make a plan

Making an essay plan may not earn you any marks but it does enable you to write a better answer and improves your chances of a higher grade. There is no standard or expected way to do a plan – you need to experiment with different ways of planning to find one that suits you.

Below is an example of one way of planning a response to the second bullet in the question above.

Pattern notes/thought mapping/spider diagrams

Start with the essence of your plan, for example the title, in the middle of the diagram. Think of four or five key ideas and put them around the title. Add detailed references and quotations to your key ideas.

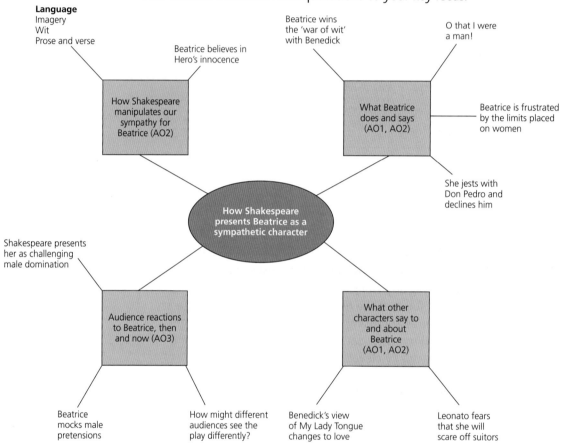

When you have mapped out your ideas and the evidence for the points you could make, as shown above, decide on the best order for your ideas and major points to make a definite line of argument. There is no need to rewrite your plan – just number the ideas and points in sequence. Start with the best point for an introduction and think how you will conclude with a reference back to the title.

Whichever style of planning you prefer, once you have planned out what you want to say you can concentrate on saying it well. You should say what you think, so don't be afraid to write 'I think that…'. However, you should avoid the kind of casual informal language you might use in a text or a chat with a friend. Stick to 'Shakespeare' rather than Will or Bill! Use clear standard English, as if you were writing for your English teacher.

GRADE BOOSTER

```
Do not lose sight of the playwright in your essay.
Remember that Much Ado About Nothing is a construct —
the characters, their thoughts, their words, their
actions have all been created by Shakespeare — so
most of your points need to be about what Shakespeare
might have been trying to achieve. In explaining
how his message is conveyed, for instance through an
event, something about a character, use of imagery,
personification, or irony, don't forget to mention
his name.
For example:
```

- Shakespeare makes it clear that…
- It is evident from… that Shakespeare is inviting the audience to consider…
- Here, the audience may well feel that Shakespeare is suggesting…

How to make your argument clear

Try to make sure that the examiner can hear what you were thinking by reading what you have written. It can be helpful to signpost your line of argument by using discourse markers – terms and phrases such as these:

- firstly
- although
- consequently
- nevertheless
- but the original audience might have felt
- however
- on the other hand
- an alternative view would be that
- finally

Merely asserting your personal point of view will not gain you many marks – you always need to cite evidence from the play for the points you make and then go on to explore and analyse that evidence (see 'Sample essays' on p. 79 for examples of answers that do this).

GRADE BOOSTER

```
If you can't decide whether a phrase is a simile or a
metaphor, you can still refer to it as an example of
imagery.
```

Writing in an appropriate style

Remember that you are expected to write in a suitable register. This means that you need to use an appropriate style. This means:

- Not using colloquial language or slang unless quoting from the text, e.g. 'Don John is a nasty piece of work. A bit of a toe-rag really.'
- Not becoming too personal, e.g. 'Leonato is like my dad, right, 'cos he…'
- Not being too dogmatic. Don't say 'This means that…'. It is much better to say 'This might suggest that…'
- Using suitable phrases for an academic essay, e.g. 'It could be argued that', not 'I reckon that…'

How to use quotations

Except when writing about an extract that is before you on the exam paper you can use quotations only if you can remember them. That alone should convince you that short quotations are better than long ones, but there are other good reasons for keeping quotations brief.

Short quotations are better because they:

- are quick to write down
- can clinch your point quickly
- leave you time to explore your ideas
- gain as much credit as longer quotations
- reveal your knowledge of the play rapidly
- show that you can select judiciously from the text

Rather than trying to remember long quotations it is easier, and more effective, to remember key words and/or very short phrases and use these 'mini quotations' to clinch the points you make.

Look through the (long) quotations below and try to select from them 'mini quotations' (key words or short phrases) which you could use to fill in the blanks in the paragraph about Leonato that follows.

> Daughter, remember what I told you: if the prince do solicit you in that kind, you know your answer.
>
> (2.1 48)

> Do not live, Hero, do not ope thine eyes:
> For did I think thou wouldst not quickly die,
> Thought I thy spirits were stronger than thy shames,
> Myself would on the rearward of reproaches
> Strike at thy life.
>
> (4.1 116–120)

oh she is fallen
Into a pit of ink that the wide sea
Hath drops too few to wash her clean again.

(4.1 132)

Leonato is not presented as a caring father: he sees Hero almost
as a piece of property to be disposed of. He shows no concern for
her feelings when he says that if the Prince should seek her hand,
'_____.' His belief in her guilt is immediate, and his
command to his daughter is, '_____.' His concern is
only for the stain on his own reputation when he says she has
fallen '_____.'

GRADE BOOSTER

```
It is important to make the individual quotations
you select brief and to try to embed them. This will
save you time, enabling you to develop your points at
greater depth and so raise your grade.
```

Key points to remember

- Do not just jump straight in. Spending time wisely in those first moments may gain you extra marks later.
- Write a brief plan.
- Remember to answer the question.
- Refer closely to details in the passage in your answer, support your comments, and remember you must also refer to the play as a whole (or refer to 'elsewhere' in the play for Edexcel and WJEC/Eduqas).
- Use your time wisely. Try to leave a few minutes to look back over your work and check your spelling, punctuation and grammar, so that your meaning is clear and so that you know that have done the very best that you can.
- Keep an eye on the clock.

Examining the text

You will be examined on Shakespeare's text, so it is important for you to examine the text for yourself. The exam questions are really about Shakespeare as a dramatist, and the text of the play is what you have as evidence for what you say.

As you get to know the play better, ask yourself a series of questions about Shakespeare's reasons for writing each scene as he did:

1 Why did Shakespeare include this scene at this point in the play?
2 What did Shakespeare choose to have happen on stage?

3 How does this scene contribute to the development of the plot?

4 What do we learn about the characters from this scene?

5 What mental images are conjured up by the words? How do they link with images and ideas from elsewhere?

6 What challenges face the actors in this scene?

7 How might Shakespeare have expected his audience to react to this scene?

8 What aspects of the scene have relevance today?

9 How effective do you think Shakespeare was in conveying his intentions to his audience in this scene?

10 What would be lost if this scene did not exist?

GRADE *FOCUS*

Grade 5

Grade 5 candidates:

- Have a clear focus on the text and the task and are able to 'read between the lines'.
- Develop a clear understanding of the ways in which writers use language, form and structure to create effects for the readers.
- Use a range of detailed textual evidence to support comments.
- Show understanding of the idea that both writers and audiences may be influenced by where, when and why a text is produced.

Grade 8

Grade 8 candidates:

- Produce a consistently convincing, informed response to a range of meanings and ideas within the text.
- Use ideas which are well-linked and will often build on one another.
- Dig deeply into the text, examining, exploring and evaluating writers' use of language, form and structure.
- Carefully select finely judged textual references which are well integrated in order to support and develop responses to texts.
- Show perceptive understanding of how contexts shape texts and responses to texts.

Achieving a Grade 9

To reach the very highest level you need to have thought about the play more deeply and produce a response which is conceptualised, critical and exploratory at a deeper level. You might, for instance, challenge accepted critical views in evaluating whether Shakespeare has always been successful.

You may feel that the portrayal of Hero as a passive figure could alienate some modern audiences. If so, do you consider this a problem or not? You need to make original points clearly and succinctly and convince the examiner that your viewpoint is really your own, and a valid one, with constant and careful reference to the text. This will be aided by the use of short and apposite (really relevant) quotations, skilfully embedded in your answer along the way (see 'Sample essays' on p. 79).

How to prepare well for the Shakespeare question

- Know the text of the whole play, not just parts.
- Compare different stage or screen performances of *Much Ado About Nothing*.
- Become familiar with the style and format of the questions on extracts and on the play as a whole and practise answering questions in the time allowed.
- Learn five to ten really important quotations by heart and know what points you could make about them in connection with the most important themes.
- Practise creating plans for answers in five minutes because you will need to do that in the exam.
- Be ready to write about Shakespeare's choice and use of language, and how language might affect an audience.
- Be ready to write about Shakespeare's use of characters, structure or form in a way that conveys your personal response to the play.
- Refer in your answers to the context in which the play was written.
- Make sure that you are comfortable using critical terms (e.g. *imagery*, *soliloquy* or *genre*) which enable you to write with economy and style.
- Keep the audience in mind, and remember that the attitudes of Shakespeare's audience would be different from those of a modern audience.

REVIEW YOUR LEARNING

(Answers are given on p. 103.)

1 What is the format of the Shakespeare question for the board you are sitting?
2 Which Assessment Objectives are targeted in the question for your board?
3 How long do you have to produce your response on Shakespeare?
4 Can you take a copy of the play into the examination?
5 What should you do in the first ten minutes of the Shakespeare paper?
6 How can you signal the line of your argument?
7 Why are short quotations more effective than long ones?
8 How can you use the last few minutes valuably in the exam?

Assessment Objectives and skills

All GCSE English Literature courses are designed to assess how well you read, understand and respond to literary texts. Most of *what* is to be assessed and *how* it is assessed, has been specified at national level through what are known as Assessment Objectives (AOs). This explains why the exam boards have such similar approaches. Nevertheless there are some variations in the way Shakespeare is assessed so you need to check the table below to make sure that you know how the board you will be sitting has framed the assessment.

The national objectives for reading, understanding and responding to texts are given below, along with their overall weightings for AQA, which is one of the two boards to assess all four AOs through Shakespeare.

	Read, understand and respond to texts. Students should be able to:
AO1 15%	• maintain a critical style and develop an informed personal response • use textual references, including quotations, to support and illustrate interpretations.
AO2 15%	Analyse the language, form and structure used by a writer to create meanings and effects, using relevant subject terminology where appropriate.
AO3 7.5%	Show understanding of the relationships between texts and the contexts in which they were written.
AO4 2.5%	Use a range of vocabulary and sentence structures for clarity, purpose and effect, with accurate spelling and punctuation.

The table below shows which Assessment Objectives are examined in the Shakespeare papers of the different boards.

AQA	WJEC/Eduqas	Edexcel	OCR
AO1	AO1	AO1	AO1
AO2	AO2	AO2	AO2
AO3		AO3	AO3
AO4	AO4		AO4

As you will see from the AQA weightings above, which are typical of other boards, the two objectives that carry the most marks are AO2 analysing a writer's methods (i.e. language, form and structure) and AO1 developing your personal response. Showing that you understand how the context relates to your text, if it is assessed through the Shakespeare question, carries fewer marks and the accuracy with which you write carries a maximum of 5%. That does not mean that some of the Assessment Objectives do not matter – you need every mark you can get – but it does mean that you need to prepare yourself as thoroughly as possible to write about your response to the play and to analyse Shakespeare's methods.

What skills do you need to show?

There is no secret about how to do well on the Shakespeare question. You just need to demonstrate the skills that the examiners are looking for, which are outlined in the Assessment Objectives. Below is an explanation in student-speak of what the teacher-speak of the Assessment Objectives really means.

> **AO1** Read, understand and respond to texts. Students should be able to:
> - maintain a critical style and develop an informed personal response
> - use textual references, including quotations, to support and illustrate interpretations.

At its most basic level, this AO is about having a good grasp of what a text is about and being able to express an opinion about it within the context of the question. For example, if you were to say: 'The play is about two pairs of lovers who finish up marrying' you would be beginning to address AO1 because you have made a personal response.

The word '**develop**' tells you that it is not enough to scribble down points as they occur to you. You need to build an argument, based on evidence, which is a clear response to the task set. An '**informed**' response refers to the basis on which you make that response. In other words, you need to show that you know the play well enough to answer the question.

This is closely linked to the idea that you are also required to '**use textual references including quotations to support and illustrate interpretations**'. This means giving short direct quotations from the text as suggested on pp. 70–71 in the 'Tackling the exams' section and where possible embedding them in the flow of your answer. Quotations on their own do not gain marks – they need to be there because they offer support for your developing line of argument. Sometimes it is better to refer to an event than to give a quotation (e.g. it is quicker to refer to 'the gulling scene' than to include quotations proving that Benedick was hiding behind the arbour).

Generally speaking, most candidates find AO1 relatively easy. Remember that you are writing for an examiner – someone you do not know, but who knows *Much Ado About Nothing* well and will expect to read responses in standard English. Avoid re-telling the story – there are no marks for doing that. Storytelling signals to the examiner that you do not realise that '**a critical style**' means offering thoughts and opinions about a text rather than just saying what happens in the text.

AO2 Analyse the language, form and structure used by a writer to create meanings and effects using relevant subject terminology where appropriate.

This AO focuses on how Shakespeare as a playwright has communicated his meanings to the audience. Most examiners would probably agree that covering AO2 is a weakness for many candidates, particularly those students who only ever write about the characters as if they were real people.

- **Language:** language encompasses a wide range of writers' methods, such as the use of different types of imagery, words which create sound effects, similes, irony and so on. AO2 also refers to your use of '**subject terminology**'. This means that you should be able to use terms such as *metaphor*, *alliteration* and *soliloquy* with confidence and understanding. However, if you can't remember the term, don't despair – you can still gain marks for explaining the effects being created. The best way to gain high marks on almost any Literature question is to write well about specific words that the author chose to use and the likely impact on readers. In the most well-known example, Shakespeare plants the early image of Claudio as being as 'civil as an orange' which gives greater resonance and impact to Claudio's later snarl, 'Give not this rotten orange to your friend.'

- **Form:** you need to keep in mind that Shakespeare was writing a play with an audience in mind, and to refer to this whenever appropriate.

- **Structure:** this is about the play's construction: why the events are in the sequence they are in; how themes feature; why events happen as they do and how the plot is built up. For example, Shakespeare has Dogberry and Verges and the Watch discover Don John's plot almost as soon as it has happened, thereby ensuring that the audience can hope that all will be well in the end. Another example is that as soon as Beatrice and Benedick appear and start sniping at each other verbally the audience would assume that eventually they will marry each other, and that the fun would come from seeing how this union of antagonists was brought about.

- **Use relevant subject terminology:** this part of AO2 is about the economy and effectiveness of your writing. Imagine that you are writing for your English teacher and use some of the key critical terms (e.g. *context*, *imagery* or *soliloquy*) that he or she has taught to your class. Such terms are 'shorthand' to scaffold your ideas, to make your writing more economical and give it greater precision.

| AO3 | Show understanding of the relationships between texts and the contexts in which they were written. |

'**Context**' is a word with multiple meanings which are unpicked for you on p. 10 in the 'Contexts' section. This AO is about how time and place affect the writer and audiences in different times. You need to show that you know when the play was written and how the fact that Shakespeare was an Elizabethan playwright might have influenced how he wrote.

It also means demonstrating that you understand how the original audience might have reacted to the play and how their reactions might differ from those of a modern audience.

| AO4 | Use a range of vocabulary and sentence structures for clarity, purpose and effect, with accurate spelling and punctuation. |

The way you write does matter. As examiners read your response they form impressions of the mind behind your words. You want your examiner to sense that you use and interpret words well. It is possible for a candidate to think well but write badly, but you might be surprised how rarely that happens. An examiner under time pressure (and they are) might not stay patient with an illegible script or might undervalue a badly written one.

In all the boards except Edexcel there are marks available for accuracy. To gain all of them you need to spell and punctuate with consistent accuracy, and use vocabulary and varied sentence structures to convey and control meaning effectively.

GRADE BOOSTER

Just building your response around the objectives is not the key to gaining the highest grades. That approach may be given credit for its coverage but not for its creativity or originality. Instead try to offer a convincingly personal response that includes showing the skills and knowledge assessed by the objectives. It should be automatic for you to address language, form, structure and context whilst you concentrate on how your argument answers the task.

How can you prepare yourself for meeting the objectives?

Below are ways of making it second nature to address the objectives in your writing:

- Working with a partner, look at a range of questions from past papers on *Much Ado About Nothing* and on other Shakespeare plays and try to identify where and how the objectives are targeted. (Check with your teacher if you can.)
- It takes only five minutes to create a plan, so do plenty of them as practice. Develop the habit of planning your responses with the objectives as part of your planning process. (See pp. 67–68 in the 'Tackling the exams' section.)
- Practise timed answers until you know the objectives by heart.

REVIEW YOUR LEARNING

(Answers are given on p. 104.)

1 Which Assessment Objectives does your board assess through the Shakespeare paper?
2 Which Assessment Objectives usually carry the most marks?
3 What does AO1 assess?
4 What does AO2 assess?
5 What does AO3 assess?
6 What does AO4 assess?

Sample essays

Thinking about sample answers is a good way to get your head round what examiners give marks for. Assessing sample answers against your board's criteria will help you to assess your own practice answers.

Before reading any more of this section make sure that you have read the 'Tackling the exams' and 'Assessment Objectives and Skills' sections on how to plan and write answers and how to understand the Assessment Objectives.

Bear in mind that most boards will require you to write in detail about an extract from *Much Ado About Nothing* and to write more generally about the play as a whole. AQA assesses your answers together, but some boards assess skills differently in the different parts of their questions.

Below are two answers to the same question. The question is in AQA style but the evidence which gains marks is similar across the boards.

Question 1

Read the following extract from Act 2 scene 1 of *Much Ado About Nothing* and then answer the question that follows.

At this point in the play Beatrice is dancing with Benedick at the masked ball in Leonato's house. Both are disguised.

BEATRICE

Will you not tell me who told you so?

BENEDICK

No, you shall pardon me.

BEATRICE

Nor will you not tell me who you are?

BENEDICK

Not now.

BEATRICE

That I was disdainful, and that I had my good wit out of *The Hundred Merry Tales*: well, this was Signor Benedick that said so.

BENEDICK

What's he?

BEATRICE

I am sure you know him well enough.

BENEDICK

Not I, believe me.

BEATRICE

Did he never make you laugh?

BENEDICK

I pray you, what is he?

BEATRICE

Why, he is the prince's jester: a very dull fool, only his gift is, in devising impossible slanders: none but libertines delight in him, and the commendation is not in his wit, but in his villainy, for he both pleases men and angers them, and then they laugh at him and beat him: I am sure he is in the fleet, I would he had boarded me.

BENEDICK

When I know the gentleman, I'll tell him what you say.

Starting with this conversation, explore how Shakespeare presents the relationship between Beatrice and Benedick in *Much Ado About Nothing*.

Write about:

- what Beatrice and Benedick say to each other in this conversation
- how Shakespeare presents their relationship in the play as a whole.

[30 + 4 marks]

You will see below extracts from exam responses from two students working at different levels. They cover much the same points. However, if you look carefully you will be able to see how Student B takes similar material to that of Student A, but develops it further in order to achieve a higher grade.

Student A, who is likely to achieve Grade 5, begins the response like this:

1 There are no marks for this kind of introduction since it is merely a repetition of the question.

3 Awareness of style of dialogue.

5 Shows awareness of stage context.

7 Correct use of terminology, but identifying rather than exploring.

> I am going to write about how Shakespeare presents the relationship between Beatrice and Benedick in this extract, and then in the play as a whole. The extract is in prose which is normal for these characters and the quick questioning of each other is quite entertaining for the audience since, although they pretend otherwise, (will you not tell me who you are?) we know that they do really know each other. There will be a lot of 'stage business' going on for the audience to enjoy as Benedick winces at Beatrice's description of him as 'the prince's jester.' As usual with these two there is a sexual side to their imagery – Beatrice talks naughtily of being 'boarded' by Benedick. Beatrice also uses antithesis in describing Benedick when she says, 'he both pleases men and angers them, and then they laugh at him and beat him.'

2 A valid comment but needs expanding to consider dramatic effect.

4 Appropriate focus on audience reaction.

6 Engages with language in some detail.

8 Not much mention of Shakespeare's methods apart from the opening sentence.

Student B, who is likely to achieve Grade 8, begins like this:

1 Immediate identification of the dramatic effect created by Shakespeare.

3 Awareness of stage situation in relation to the author's intentions.

> Beatrice's opening words are the continuation of a conversation the audience has not heard. Shakespeare creates the sense of a swirling dance with snatches of conversation between different masked couples. There is no great emotion here, merely social banter which is fittingly in prose. Clearly Benedick (who is recognised despite his mask in yet another twist to the theme of deception) has commented adversely on the quality of Beatrice's wit since she is insulted by the claim that, 'I had my good wit out of The Hundred Merry Tales.' The quickfire questioning of identity is also a continuation of the 'war of wit' between Beatrice and Benedick and this is reflected in the military imagery of the fleet. As usual Shakespeare shows Beatrice getting the

2 Appreciation of Shakespeare's linguistic choices.

4 Interpretation of character.

5 Linking particular words with wider aspects of the play.

6 Awareness of playwright's choices in relation to words and characters.

better of Benedick in their verbal warfare – he lays himself open with the question 'what is he?' and Beatrice launches into a devastating response – 'Why he is the prince's jester, a very dull fool.' She continues to beat him verbally with antithetical insults – 'he both pleases men and he angers them, and then they laugh at him and beat him.' There is often a sexual undercurrent to their exchanges but when Beatrice utters the risqué thought, 'I wish he had boarded me' Benedick is so deflated by what he has heard that he answers lamely, 'I'll tell him what you say.' Another round to Beatrice, who never admits that she knows she is talking with Benedick although (appropriately for a play about multiple layers of deception) their disguises are so transparent to the audience and to each other.

7 Stylish use of subject terminology.

8 Shows understanding of double meanings.

9 Sensitivity of response to language.

10 Economical and lively expression with awareness of audience and theme.

Student A has made a start that suggests that he or she is working at Grade 5 and is demonstrating 'clear understanding'. The opening section is focused on the task and there is implicit awareness of Shakespeare's methods and their effects on the audience though these are not always fully explained.

Student B has produced a better introduction with effective analysis of Shakespeare's methods and intentions. This suggests that he or she is working at Grade 8. Look back carefully and see if you can identify the differences between the openings of the two responses.

Both students broaden out their answers to the play as a whole.

Student A writes:

1 'Interesting' is not a useful critical term.

2 Effective incorporation of quotation.

Beatrice's attitude towards Benedick has always been interesting. Even before he appears on stage the messenger comments that Benedick 'is not in your books.' Beatrice's 'I wonder that you will still be talking, Signor Benedick, nobody marks you' is followed by Benedick's riposte – 'What my dear Lady Disdain! Are you yet living?' Their verbal daggers are drawn and later Benedick claims that every word is a wound – 'she speaks

3 The quotations are relevant but not sufficiently explained.

4 More focus on what the relationship is than how it is presented.

6 Clear understanding and some exploration of effect.

> poniards, every word stabs.' Beatrice declares, 'I had rather hear my dog bark at a crow than a man swear he loves me' and Benedick declares that he will never be 'Benedick the married man.' From the audience's point of view there is never much doubt that the two will end up marrying each other and an Elizabethan audience would already have recognised this. It emerges that her relationship with Benedick goes back some way when she says, 'I know you of old'.
>
> The relationship between Beatrice and Benedick is transformed during the scene in the arbour. Benedick is initially astonished at news of Beatrice's secret affection for him – 'Is't possible? Sits the wind in that corner?' but Shakespeare makes his conversion hilariously rapid once he decides 'This can be no trick.' He becomes determined 'to be horribly in love with her' although he has 'railed so long against marriage'. Beatrice's experience is a parallel, but in verse rather than prose.

5 Awareness of Shakespeare's audience.

7 Point supported by relevant quotation.

8 Almost a good point, but needed to consider impact.

This response by Student A has merit – there is clear understanding of the characters and apt quotations are incorporated into the essay – but it is more an account than an analysis. Comment is on the level of character rather than on the writer's methods and intentions. A Grade 5 remains a possibility but is not yet secure.

Student B covers similar material, but with deeper analysis:

> This brief conversation, where feelings are literally masked, is typical of the way Shakespeare presents the relationship between Beatrice and Benedick in the play as a whole: they feign one thing and feel another. From the beginning there is an element of disguise in Beatrice's stance towards Benedick which puts questions in the mind of the audience. Shakespeare has her scorning him even before

1 Stylishly effective analysis.

2 Thoughtful awareness of likely audience response.

he appears, apparently out of dislike, since the messenger comments that Benedick 'is not in your books', yet we note that he is always at the centre of her thoughts.

3 Intelligent interpretation of character based on textual evidence.

Their verbal skirmishing starts immediately with Beatrice's waspish, 'I wonder that you will still be talking, Signor Benedick, nobody marks you.' Benedick's riposte is equally barbed, 'What my dear Lady Disdain! Are you yet living?' This antagonism is so instant and so extreme that it signals to the audience that there will be much merriment in watching such loathing be transformed into loving. Later Shakespeare has Benedick make the 'merry war' between them very evident when he claims that every word is a wound – 'she speaks poniards, every word stabs.' Beatrice makes her alleged feelings plain with the amusingly exaggerated countryside image of, 'I had rather hear my dog bark at a crow than a man swear he loves me' and Benedick makes a matching declaration, noted by the audience, that he will never be 'Benedick the married man.' A later reference to Benedick having won Beatrice's heart 'with false dice' again suggests that their relationship had once been amorous rather than antagonistic.

4 Detailed comment on the effect of words.

5 More comment on words with awareness of the play's structure.

Shakespeare uses deceit to reveal the truth of the characters' feelings for each other in the arbour scene. Despite his reputation of being a 'professed tyrant' to women, Benedick is shown as determined to be 'horribly in love' with Beatrice. The falsehoods of others reveal a hidden truth – they are right for each other and do love each other. The moment when this is confirmed is significant in terms of the structural patterning of characters – Benedick puts love before friendship in agreeing to challenge Claudio. From the audience's point of view there is never much doubt that the two will end up marrying each other – it is the main driver of the comic plot, and an Elizabethan audience would have recognised that early on.

6 Analysis of Shakespeare's methods.

7 Analysis of structure.

8 Informed by appreciation of context.

Sample response B is demonstrating qualities that meet the criteria for a Grade 8 by incorporating textual evidence effectively and analysing Shakespeare's methods in a thoughtfully developed way.

Sample response A concludes as follows:

> Both characters are shown as bewildered but amused by their new-found love – Benedick says, 'I do love nothing in the world so well as you, is not that strange?' Beatrice's response is similar – 'As strange as the thing I know not.' The test of their love comes with Beatrice's command to 'Kill Claudio' after the way he has shamed Hero, and Benedick's love passes that test.
>
> Shakespeare contrasts Beatrice and Benedick's unconventional relationship with the much more conventional relationship between Hero and Claudio, but both end in marriage in accord with comic convention.

1 Point supported by textual evidence.

2 Solid grasp of the details of the play as a whole.

3 Understanding of structure in the patterning of characters.

4 Concludes with appropriate reference to literary convention.

This is the conclusion of sample response B:

> These two characters, invented by Shakespeare rather than found in the sources, are the comic heart of the play. However, since nothing is what it seems in Messina, the relationship between Beatrice and Benedick which appears impossible becomes inevitable. The relationship is presented not just through characters' words and actions but also through the pattern of the play's structure.
>
> Shakespeare did not present Beatrice and Benedick in isolation: he created the quartet of main characters as two contrasting pairs with Beatrice and Benedick shown as more intelligent, more sophisticated and more voluble than Claudio and Hero. The older pair are entertainingly unconventional. In part this may

1 Informed reference to sources.

2 Economical analysis of key theme.

3 Explicit concern with structure.

4 Explores the significance of character patterning.

be because both are presented as individuals on the edge of their social groups rather than at the centre of them and are consequently presented as freer from conventional social constraints.

5 Thoughtful analysis.

6 Sophisticated interpretation.

As an audience we are invited to operate a 'willing suspension of disbelief' over the way both characters discover love through the deceit of the gulling scenes. This is made dramatically acceptable by the way both characters voice their wonder at what has happened – Benedick's, 'I do love nothing in the world so well as you, is not that strange?' is matched by Beatrice's response – 'As strange as the thing I know not.'

7 Maintains awareness of dramatic context and audience response.

When, inevitably, the two agree to marry, the tone of mockery is continued, with the abstract nouns reason, persuasion and pity cited as justifications for emotion. Beatrice admits to loving Benedick 'no more than reason' and yields only 'upon great persuasion,' whilst Benedick declares, 'I take thee for pity.' This is not the conventional language of love, but as a consequence it is all the more convincing as evidence of the depth of their relationship. Beatrice and Benedick so enrich the play through their witty exchanges that we feel early on as an audience that this will not end in tragedy – the ending Shakespeare wanted us care about is the comic union of the two who declared their hatred of marrying and of each other.

8 Detailed and perceptive linguistic analysis.

9 Confident conclusion with authorial intention in mind.

Student A's conclusion has limitations but does merit a Grade 5 since it offers a coherent response based on relevant evidence. There is examination of Shakespeare's language and structure and some consideration of his methods.

Student B's conclusion deserves Grade 8 because it offers convincing critical analysis and exploration, is grounded in textual detail and explores the effects of Shakespeare's methods. Contextual factors are taken into account in relation to the author's intentions. It is written with style and shows sophisticated insight.

The following sample responses are based on an extract question which focuses on theme, rather than character. The format for the question is as for WJEC/Eduqas, but the marking criteria are similar for other boards.

Question 2

Answer both part (a) and part (b).

You are advised to spend about 20 minutes on part (a), and about 40 minutes on part (b).

(a) Read the extract below.

How does Shakespeare create tension for an audience here? Refer closely to details from the extract to support your answer.

[15 marks]

*(b) How does Shakespeare present male attitudes to women in *Much Ado About Nothing*? [25 marks]

5 of this question's marks are allocated for accuracy in spelling, punctuation and the use of vocabulary and sentence structures.

CLAUDIO

Stand thee by, friar: father, by your leave,

Will you with free and unconstrained soul

Give me this maid your daughter?

LEONATO

As freely, son, as God did give her me.

CLAUDIO

And what have I to give you back, whose worth

May counterpoise this rich and precious gift?

DON PEDRO

Nothing, unless you render her again.

CLAUDIO

Sweet prince, you learn me noble thankfulness:

There, Leonato, take her back again,

Give not this rotten orange to your friend,

She's but the sign and semblance of her honour:

Behold how like a maid she blushes here!

Oh what authority and show of truth

Can cunning sin cover itself withal!

Comes not that blood, as modest evidence,

To witness simple virtue? Would you not swear

All you that see her, that she were a maid,

By these exterior shows? But she is none:

She knows the heat of a luxurious bed:

Her blush is guiltiness, not modesty.

LEONATO

What do you mean, my lord?

CLAUDIO

Not to be married,

Not to knit my soul to an approved wanton.

Below is what Student X, who is hoping to achieve Grade 5, wrote in answer to the part (a) question:

There is plenty of tension in this passage because although we know that Borachio's plot has been discovered, Claudio doesn't. Claudio's behaviour in church has been strange, starting with a rude 'No' when asked if he has come to marry Hero and exploding with sneering rage about 'what men dare do!'. Claudio speaks to the friar and then calmly asks Leonato whether he will 'give me this maid your daughter?' There is less tension when Claudio asks what he could give back for such a 'rich and precious gift'.

After thanking the prince Claudio is then deliberately vicious in returning Hero as a 'rotten orange'. His fury builds as he declares that she is 'but the sign and semblance of her honour.' His dark mood culminates in 'Not to be married, Not to knit my soul to an approved wanton.'

The audience is less bewildered than Leonato and the others, because we know more of the situation, but there is still considerable dramatic tension: we do not know how things will develop. We have yet to hear Hero and an audience might think that in this mood Claudio could possibly kill her.

1 Gets straight to the point.

2 Shows awareness of the events surrounding the extract, putting it accurately into context.

3 Shows understanding of situation on stage.

4 Appropriate use of textual support, with well embedded quotation.

5 Remember to keep quotations, especially from a given extract, short and to the point.

6 Some awareness of the effect of language, but too little explicit analysis.

7 Begins to interpret, but has not mentioned Shakespeare.

This response merits consideration for Grade 5 because it comments coherently on and begins to analyse Shakespeare's methods, makes some reference to meanings and effects, and includes direct reference to the text.

Below is what Student Y, who is hoping to achieve Grade 8, wrote in answer to the part (a) question:

As members of an audience we know that we are watching a comedy yet this moment is full of uncertainty and potentially tragic tension. Shakespeare has shown us how Claudio has been deceived and shown us his intention to shame Hero in the church. We also know that Borachio's plot has been discovered, but there is a real danger that since the emergence of the truth depends on the Watch, Claudio might do more than shame Hero.

Claudio's behaviour in church has been strange as Benedick notes in response to Claudio's outburst, 'O what men dare do!' Depending on how it is played, there could be a normality about Claudio's first speech in the extract that keeps the audience guessing: he dismisses the friar and then asks a reasonable-sounding question of Leonato — whether he will 'give me this maid your daughter?' This could be spoken naturally or snarled with barely-contained menace, but the tension lessens temporarily as Claudio asks what he could give back for such a 'rich and precious gift'.

After thanking the prince Claudio is deliberately vicious in returning Hero as a 'rotten orange', an image of inner decay and foulness. His fury builds to a crescendo of curse-like alliteration declaring that she is 'but the sign and semblance of her honour' and proclaiming, with a rare degree of dramatic irony, what pretence 'can cunning sin cover itself withal.' Central to the theme of deception is that he is right about the concealment but wrong about the culprit. The negativity of his mood is reflected in the 'not… not…none' of the next few lines that culminate in 'Not to be married, Not to knit my soul to an approved wanton.'

1 Precise location of the extract and perceptive analysis of likely audience reaction.

2 Explicit recognition of author's intentions.

3 Apt and relevant quotation from outside the extract.

4 Awareness of alternative interpretations.

5 Accurate use of subject terminology.

6 Appreciation of Shakespeare's methods.

7 Analysis of ideas.

8 Detailed analysis of the effects of word choice.

The audience is less bewildered than Leonato and the others, because we know more of the situation, but there is still considerable dramatic tension: we do not know how things will develop. We have yet to hear from Hero and in this mood Claudio seems capable of anything.

9 Appreciation of the dramatic impact of the moment.

This response is worthy of Grade 8 because it sustains focus on the task, shows perceptive understanding, uses precise subject terminology to analyse Shakespeare's methods, makes assured reference to meanings and effects and evaluates the way meaning and ideas are conveyed.

Below is Student X's answer to the part (b) question:

The play as a whole makes us question relationships between the sexes because there are no stupid women but there are lots of stupid men, and they are the ones in charge.

1 Forthright initial overview.

Leonato gives away his daughter as if she was a piece of cake – ('Count, take of me my daughter'). Don Pedro thinks it OK to woo a woman and then hand her over to another man. Borachio assumes that he can easily manipulate Margaret. Claudio's attitudes show through his words: he calls Hero a 'jewel', and he loves what she looks like rather than what she is. ('In mine eye she is the sweetest lady that ever I looked on.')

2 Interpretation clinched with quotation.

3 Shows secure understanding of key aspects of the text.

4 Detailed analysis of language.

Claudio feels justified in humiliating Hero because he thinks she has sullied his masculine honour. The most powerful moment of the main plot is when Claudio stands snarling at a silent Hero – 'She knows the heat of a luxurious bed. Her blush is guiltiness not modesty.' What audience would not find this cruelty a condemnation of male attitudes?

5 Shows understanding of the text, offering a personal response.

6 Reference to meanings and effects conveyed through language.

Leonato finds it hard to believe that his (male) social superiors could be wrong, but once Don John's plot is revealed the Count and Claudio sort of shrink before your eyes. This 'pair

7 Sustained focus on the task, conveying ideas with coherence and often (but not always) using an appropriate register.

of honourable men' in Leonato's words, are completely humbled: Claudio says, 'Impose me to what penance your invention can lay upon my sin' whilst Don Pedro says he would 'bend under any weight'.

Benedick moves from being 'a professed tyrant' to 'the fair sex' to becoming (as we all knew he would!) 'a married man', which gives the lie to the life of a bachelor being the bees' knees. The unmarried Duke is a forlorn figure at the end.

Through both plots Shakespeare challenges men's attitudes to women. By the end of the play modern audiences tend to wonder whether a man like Claudio deserves a woman like Hero, rather than the other way round.

9 Evaluates the way meaning and ideas are conveyed through structure and form.

8 Shows secure understanding of key aspects of the text.

10 Awareness of audience response.

The response above has definite strengths as well as limitations (AO2 could be stronger). It could just merit consideration for Grade 5. Below is another answer to the part (b) question, drawing on the same materials but written by Student Y who is hoping for a Grade 8:

Shakespeare's male characters show typical Elizabethan attitudes to women: Messina is a male-dominated world in which fathers control their daughters' destinies and in general women should be seen but not heard. For example, Leonato is embarrassed by Beatrice's witty loquacity and her mockery of martial valour with its accompanying male virtues. He warns her, 'thou wilt never get thee a husband if thou be so shrewd of thy tongue.' Nevertheless the play as a whole challenges these attitudes and makes us question relationships between the sexes. There is no female equivalent of Don John's evil, nor of Dogberry's foolishness. Apart from Margaret, who seems unaware of how she risks Hero's good name, Shakespeare makes the female characters more admirable than the male.

1 Intelligent initial overview showing awareness of the historical context.

Leonato jokes crudely about his wife's fidelity and readily gives away his daughter in marriage ('Count, take of me my daughter'). We remember this later when his regret is more for himself than for his slandered daughter. Don Pedro pulls rank to woo Hero successfully, only to hand her over to another man and Borachio assumes, rightly, that he can manipulate Margaret. Claudio's attitudes show through his words: he calls Hero a 'jewel', equating her with a pretty, precious object rather than a human being and says, 'Let every eye negotiate for itself'. He is using the language of the marketplace about something that can be bought and sold for a price. He loves with his eyes rather than his heart ('In mine eye she is the sweetest lady that ever I looked on') and this love of appearances proves all too vulnerable to malicious deceit.

Claudio is shown as feeling justified in humiliating Hero because his manly honour has, he thinks, been besmirched. The most powerful dramatic moment of the main plot is when he stands snarling abuse at a silent Hero – 'She knows the heat of a luxurious bed. Her blush is guiltiness not modesty.' How is Hero shown to retaliate? In the only ways traditionally possible – passive, silent suffering and eventual collapse. By contrast, Beatrice's immediate anger with Claudio is a sign of her emotional strength, but also of her social and physical weakness, since despite her fury she still needs Benedick as a male champion to tackle Claudio – 'O God that I were a man! I would eat his heart in the marketplace.' At this point Shakespeare gives her words and attitudes traditionally associated with males but her actions are constrained by convention. The audience already knows that the accusations are false so is Shakespeare inviting his audience to condemn such male attitudes?

2 Interpretation clinched with quotation.

3 Shows secure understanding of key aspects of the text.

4 Detailed analysis of language and effect.

5 Shows understanding and interpretation.

6 Detailed analysis of meanings and effects conveyed through language, with intelligent tentativeness about interpretation.

7 Sustained focus on the task, conveying ideas with coherence and often (but not always) using an appropriate register.

Leonato is one of the upwardly mobile merchant class that existed in Shakespeare's day. He is obsequious towards the Prince and finds it hard to believe that his (male) social superiors could be wrong. He is portrayed as so self-centred that in his lamentations the word 'I' rings through the self-pitying lines and he is diminished in the eyes of the audience. Once Don John's plot is revealed the Count and Claudio, a 'pair of honourable men' in Leonato's words, are completely humbled. The emotional authority drains away from the Count and Claudio and rests with Hero's defenders, most notably Beatrice. Claudio says, 'Impose me to what penance your invention can lay upon my sin' whilst Don Pedro says he would 'bend under any weight.'

8 Perceptive interpretation of key aspects of the text.

Even Benedick, probably the male character most worthy of audience regard, is continually bested in witty repartee by 'My Lady Tongue' and at times he seeks to avoid Beatrice. He moves from being 'a professed tyrant' to 'the fair sex' to becoming (inevitably) 'a married man.' This gives the lie to the life of a bachelor being the ideal, and the unmarried Duke cuts a forlorn figure at the end.

9 Evaluates the way meaning and ideas are conveyed through structure and form.

The male/female situation was given an additional dimension by the fact that all the women were played by boys since women were not allowed to perform on the stage in Shakespeare's time. In both main and sub-plot Shakespeare challenges men's attitudes to women. By the end of the play modern audiences tend to wonder whether a man like Claudio deserves a woman like Hero, rather than the other way round, but Shakespeare's own view remains enigmatic.

10 Awareness of historical context and audience response.

93

The second version is clearly worthy of a Grade 8 because it sustains a coherent critical style and displays an informed personal response to the text showing consistently perceptive understanding. Textual references and quotations are precise, pertinent and skilfully embedded and there is intelligent analysis of Shakespeare's use of language, form and structure to create meanings and effects. The response shows an informed and perceptive understanding of how context informs evaluation of the text.

Top ten

As your examination will be 'closed book' and you will only have a short extract in front of you, you might find it helpful to memorise some quotations to use to support your points in the examination response, particularly when addressing the question on the play as a whole. Please see the 'Tackling the exams' section on p. 63 for further information about the format of the examination.

see the 'Tackling the exams' section on p. 63 for further information

> **GRADE BOOSTER**
>
> ```
> It will help you in the exam if you select ten
> quotations from across each of the sections to learn
> or at least paraphrase as it boosts your confidence and
> helps you organise your thoughts when planning your
> answer. You don't need to remember long quotations;
> short quotes that you can embed into a sentence will
> be far more effective. If all else fails, as long as
> you can remember the gist of what the quotation relates
> to, you can use a textual reference.
> ```

All four exam boards use extract-based questions and this is designed to help you use quotations. So if your memory fails, just select apt words or phrases from the extract as this will fulfil the part of AO1 which relates to quoting from the text, and then make textual references to other places in the play. Remember the examiner is looking for an individual, conceptualised, analytical response to the play and is not really testing your ability to learn long passages parrot-fashion.

Top ten character quotations

The following quotations can be used as a quick reminder of the way that Shakespeare has presented the key characteristics of each of the main characters.

I wonder that you will still be talking, Signor Benedick, nobody marks you. (Beatrice, 1.1 86)

1

- Beatrice's first words to Benedick signal the opening of verbal hostilities.

I am loved of all ladies, only you excepted. (Benedick, 1.1 92)

2

- This suggests that Benedick is not hostile to all women; he just doesn't love any woman enough to marry her.

3 let them signify under my sign, 'Here may you see Benedick the married man.' (Benedick, 1.1 199)

- The audience would recognise that this declaration of hostility to marriage is there to add to the merriment since Benedick is bound to marry.

4 I cannot hide what I am. (Don John, 1.3 10)

- Don John is more open than most of the other characters: he does not hide his malice from himself or from the audience.

5 oh she is fallen into a pit of ink (Leonato, 4.1 132)

- Leonato's image, with its overtones of legal documents and darkness, suggests that he is more concerned that his reputation will be stained than that his daughter has been shamed.

6 But, masters, remember that I am an ass. (Dogberry, 4.2 62–63)

- Dogberry's insistence on being 'writ down' an ass is hilarious, not least because of his pomposity.

GRADE **BOOSTER**

The most frequently used method for learning quotations is to write them down, repeat them and then test yourself. However, if you are a visual learner, you might try drawing one of these quotes with the quotation as a caption.

7 I cannot be a man with wishing, therefore I will die a woman with grieving. (Beatrice, 4.1 306)

- Beatrice's frustration at the customs and conventions that control women's lives is evident.

8 Yet sinned I not but in mistaking. (Claudio, 5.1 241)

- Claudio's plaintive excuse, seeking to justify himself, confirms his moral inadequacy in the eyes of the audience.

9 Come, I will have thee, but by this light I take thee for pity. (Benedick, 5.4 92)

- Benedick is joking here, knowing that the joke is on himself as much as on Beatrice.

I yield upon great persuasion, and partly to save your life (Beatrice, 5.4 94)

10

- Beatrice is playing the same game as Benedick – feigning reluctance in a way that convinces the audience that their love is deeper than conventional sentiments.

GRADE *BOOSTER*

If you find that you can't remember a full quotation, try and remember its main message. For example, with the last two quotations you might write that Benedick claimed to marry Beatrice for pity, and that she accepted him only after great persuasion.

Top ten thematic quotations

Appearance and reality

she is the sweetest lady that ever I looked on. (Claudio, 1.1 139)

1

- Shakespeare uses the imagery of seeing to suggest the superficiality of Claudio's love and to set the scene for the later manipulation of appearances.

If you dare not trust that you see, confess not that you know. (Don John, 3.2 88)

2

- Don John is manipulating appearances here, but Shakespeare is exploring the inadequacies of seeing and seeming.

Oh what authority and show of truth/Can cunning sin cover itself withal! (Claudio, 4.1 30–31)

3

- The irony of Claudio's words will not be lost on an audience which already knows that he has been deceived.

Women and men

Count, take of me my daughter (Leonato, 2.1 229)

4

- Leonato takes the conventional Elizabethan view that daughters' destinies can be determined by their fathers.

5 Oh God that I were a man! I would eat his heart in the market place. (Beatrice, 4.1 294)

- Beatrice's words here are violent in a way that is rare for female characters – the image of eating a pulsating heart is a disgusting one, showing her frustrated fury.

Wisdom and folly

6 Is our whole dissembly appeared? (Dogberry, 4.2 1)

- As so often Shakespeare gives Dogberry a mangled word – he means 'assembly' – yet there is truth in his question since 'dissembling' has been the crime and is a key theme of the play.

7 What your wisdoms could not discover, these shallow fools have brought to light. (Borachio, 5.1 205)

- Borachio's comment draws the audience's attention to what Shakespeare has done – shown the nobles to be inwardly more foolish than the outwardly foolish Watch.

8 Oh what men dare do! What men may do! What men daily do, not knowing what they do! (Claudio, 4.1 14–15)

- This is Claudio's folly at its height, and the dramatic irony is that what he says applies most strongly to himself.

Love and marriage

9 Would it not grieve a woman to be overmastered with a piece of valiant dust? (Beatrice, 2.1 43)

- Beatrice's rejection of marriage has imaginative depth – the idea that Man is but dust is the basis of an amusing image as the dust comes to life in the form of a husband. Here she is typically reductive about male valour.

10 Prince, thou art sad. Get thee a wife, get thee a wife! (Benedick, 5.4 114)

- This amounts to a complete reversal in attitude on Benedick's part, to the amusement of the audience.

Top ten Shakespeare's techniques quotations

Imagery

Let every eye negotiate for itself. (Claudio, 2.1 134)

- Shakespeare uses Claudio's commercial language of buying and selling to warn the audience how superficial his love will prove to be.

1

she speaks poniards, and every word stabs (Benedick, 2.1 187)

- Benedick's language is magnificently metaphorical, and here the use of military imagery (poniards are daggers) reminds us of the 'merry war' between Benedick and Beatrice.

2

what a deformed thief this fashion is (Borachio, 3.3 107)

- This personification of fashion is imaginatively amusing. It is also an image that Shakespeare's fashion-conscious Elizabethan audience would have relished.

3

civil as an orange, and something of that jealous complexion (Beatrice of Claudio, 2.1 223); Give not this rotten orange to your friend. (Claudio, 4.1 27)

- Shakespeare's repetition of the image of an orange gives it added significance.

4

Humour

I had rather hear my dog bark at a crow than a man swear he loves me. (Beatrice, 1.1 97)

- Beatrice's comparison is amusingly extreme and typical of much of the play's imagery in that it is drawn from the Elizabethan countryside.

5

6 she's too low for a high praise, too brown for a fair praise, and too little for a great praise. (Benedick, 1.1 126)

- This repetitive categorisation of Hero's faults is a typical of the way Shakespeare uses Benedick's humour to challenge the flowing, flowery falseness of the language of courtly love.

7 You have put him down, lady, you have put him down. (Don Pedro)
So I would not he should do me, my lord. (Beatrice, 2.1 214)

- Beatrice's deliberate misinterpretation of Don Pedro's words is just one example of the bawdy, sexual humour that runs throughout the play.

8 Dost thou not suspect my place? (Dogberry, 4.2 61)

- Shakespeare has Dogberry mixing up his words here – he means *respect* not *suspect* – yet as often there is sense behind the nonsense: we do suspect that someone like Dogberry should not be a constable of the Watch.

Linguistic features

9 Friendship is constant in all other things/Save in the office and affairs of love. (2.1 131)

- Shakespeare saves blank verse for moments of high emotion, as here and in the church scene.

10 Grieved I, I had but one?...Why had I one? (Leonato, 4.1 120)

- Shakespeare's use and repetition of the first person pronoun 'I' signals to the audience that Leonato cares more about his reputation than his daughter's.

Wider reading

Critical texts

- Cambridge Student Guide: *Much Ado About Nothing* by Mike Clamp (CUP, 2002: ISBN 0-521-00824-7). Perceptive scene-by-scene commentary and informative sections on Shakespeare's language and chronological context.

- York Notes (Advanced): *Much Ado About Nothing* by Ross Stuart (Pearson, 2004: ISBN 0-582-82303-X). Detailed commentary and notes on Shakespeare's life and background, plus critical comment and a useful glossary of literary terms.

- Globe Education: *Much Ado About Nothing* edited by Fiona Banks, Paul Shuter and Patrick Spottiswoode (2012: ISBN 9781444136661). An edition of the play that is invaluable for giving a sense of how the play might have been performed and how the interpretations of directors can differ.

- New Cambridge Shakespeare: *Much Ado About Nothing* edited by F. H. Mares and Angela Stock (2003: ISBN 0-521-53250-7). The introduction is particularly good on sources and on stage history. There is also a valuable section on film, stage and critical interpretations.

- Arden Shakespeare: *Much Ado About Nothing* edited by A. R. Humphreys (1981/2002: ISBN 1-903436-46-X). A scholarly introduction plus detailed and authoritative textual notes. The best place to go if you are looking for historical information on particular lines or words.

- Cambridge School Shakespeare: *Much Ado About Nothing* edited by Rex Gibson et al. (CUP, 2014: ISBN 978-1-107-61989-0). An exciting edition, amply illustrated with photographs from stage productions and full of relevant ideas and information on language, themes and performance.

Film

- Kenneth Branagh's 1993 production starring Emma Thompson and Richard Briers, among many famous others. If you have the chance to watch only one film version of *Much Ado About Nothing* make it this one, and enjoy it!

Websites

- Useful websites for students include BBC *Bitesize*, Sparknotes, eNotes and Cliffsnotes.

Answers

Answers to the 'Review your learning' sections:

Context (p. 19)

1 The historical context; the literary context; the context of the text; the audience context; the performance context.
2 See page 8.
3 More direct contact with the audience.
4 Beatrice, Benedick and Dogberry.
5 Possibly the nature of the sub-plot which Shakespeare invented.
6 There could be a case for greater sympathy with him.
7 Your choice – trust your own judgement.
8 See page 17.
9 The bawdy references are harder to understand, e.g. about cuckoldry.
10 Particularly with regard to the role of women.

Plot and structure (p. 34)

1 By introducing them as antagonists who nevertheless focus on each other.
2 Wit, intelligence and unconventionality.
3 Attitudes to marriage and parental authority.
4 Benedick's antics as he listens.
5 They often mean the opposite of what Dogberry intends.
6 A rotten orange.
7 Inexplicable evil.
8 Satirical view of society where the fools see more than the wise.
9 Well, do you?
10 No brainer!

Characterisation (p. 43)

1 By using phrases such as 'Shakespeare has X say...'
2 Your choice. Try to find quotations from the beginning, middle and end.
3 Find quotations that show him as scorning marriage, seeking marriage and finally advocating marriage.
4 Shakespeare has Hero saying comparatively little, so your quotations may be from Beatrice.

5 Verbal humour, on-stage behaviour and discovering Borachio's plot.

6 How about self-centred and a social snob?

7 One has the benefit of others in mind, the other seeks only to make mischief and cause hurt.

Themes (p. 52)

1 A theme is an idea that the playwright explores throughout a play.

2 Appearance and reality; women and men; wisdom and folly; love and marriage.

3 Choose from the text or look in the 'Top ten' section.

4 Hero faints but Beatrice fights for her cousin's innocence.

5 Possibly Dogberry setting the Watch, Claudio being deceived and Leonato believing the accusations against Hero.

6 Choose from the many to show how he moves from being anti-marriage to defending marriage.

Language, style and analysis (p. 62)

1 Act 2 scene 1 is a useful example of prose/verse switching.

2 There are hundreds to choose from. Look back to the examples given in this chapter.

3 His malapropisms are verbally very funny for audiences across times.

4 Anthithesis is balancing one part of an expression against another. There are examples in this chapter.

5 Use of double meanings to entertain the audience, e.g. Signor Mountanto.

6 Fashion is about appearance rather than substance – a key theme.

7 For example, witty Beatrice and foolish Dogberry.

8 For example, Claudio's images of buying and selling and Beatrice's use of military imagery.

Tackling the exams (p. 73)

1 This depends on the board. Check the table on page 64.

2 This depends on the board. Again, check the table on page 64.

3 This depends on the board. Check the table on page 64, but generally around 50 minutes.

4 No.

5 Read the question very carefully and produce your plan.

6 Use discourse markers as suggested on page 69.

7 They are easier to remember and quicker to write.

8 Review your answer in relation to the question.

Assessment Objectives and skills (p. 78)

1 This depends on the board. Check the table on page 74.
2 AO1 and AO2.
3 Knowledge of the play and your personal response to it.
4 The writer's use of language, structure and form.
5 Context. (See page 77.)
6 The quality of your writing.